IT'S THE **WAY** YOU SAY IT

IT'S THE **WAY** YOU SAY IT

Becoming Articulate, Well-Spoken, and Clear

CAROL A. FLEMING, PhD

BK

Berrett–Koehler Publishers, Inc.
San Francisco
a BK Life book

Berrett-Koehler Publishers, Inc.

235 Montgomery Street, Suite 650

San Francisco, CA 94104-2916

Tel: (415) 288-0260   Fax: (415) 362-2512   www.bkconnection.com

Ordering Information
Quantity sales. Special discounts are available on quantity purchases by corporations, associations, and others. For details, contact the "Special Sales Department" at the Berrett-Koehler address above.

Individual sales. Berrett-Koehler publications are available through most bookstores. They can also be ordered directly from Berrett-Koehler: Tel: (800) 929-2929; Fax: (802) 864-7626; www.bkconnection.com

Orders for college textbook/course adoption use. Please contact Berrett-Koehler: Tel: (800) 929-2929; Fax: (802) 864-7626.

Orders by U.S. trade bookstores and wholesalers. Please contact Ingram Publisher Services, Tel: (800) 509-4887; Fax: (800) 838-1149; E-mail: customer.service@ingrampublisherservices.com; or visit www.ingrampublisherservices.com/Ordering for details about electronic ordering.

Berrett-Koehler and the BK logo are registered trademarks of Berrett-Koehler Publishers, Inc.

Printed in the United States of America

Berrett-Koehler books are printed on long-lasting acid-free paper. When it is available, we choose paper that has been manufactured by environmentally responsible processes. These may include using trees grown in sustainable forests, incorporating recycled paper, minimizing chlorine in bleaching, or recycling the energy produced at the paper mill.

Cover Design: Leslie Waltzer / Crowfoot Design

Project Management: Lisa Crowder; Adept Content Solutions; Urbana, IL

Full-service book production: Adept Content Solutions; Urbana, IL

Library of Congress Cataloging-in-Publication Data

Fleming, Carol A.
  It's the way you say it : becoming articulate, well-spoken, and clear /
Carol A. Fleming, PH.D.—Second Edition.
     pages cm
  Includes index.
  ISBN 978-1-60994-743-9 (pbk.)
  1. Oral communication. I. Title.
  P95.F54 2013
  808.5—dc23
                         2012046353

Second Edition
18 17 16 15 14 13   10 9 8 7 6 5 4 3

Contents

Preface to the Second Edition

There are many people who simply cannot stand the sound of their own voice and are ashamed of the way they talk. They avoid opportunities for social conversation and presentations that would advance their careers because of their personal discomfort in just speaking to others.

Perhaps you are one of these people. If so, here is something you should know: many of the fluent, comfortable, "natural born" speakers that you hear conversing or presenting were actually terrified people who have found their way to success through appropriate training and practice.

Perhaps you can be one of those people.

In the first edition of *It's the Way You Say It*, I told the stories of my clients who were trying to deal with their personal communication issues. My readers have let me know that these stories were very important in helping them identify their own concerns and in seeing that there are actually ways of developing into more confident communicators. More stories are pouring in from around the world by phone and e-mail (a daunting example: "Dr. Fleming, I love my wife dearly, but I cannot stand the sound of her voice!"). So I am grateful indeed for this opportunity to include some of these stories in this revised edition of my book.

I am finding that the possibility of a new *hope* is the constant element in my clients and readers alike. They simply did not realize that there were things to know and do that would help them change and make a tremendous difference in their lives.

Many self-help authors have told me that they write their books in order to "drive people to their website," "to book more speaking engagements," "to increase their client base." Not me. I just want to give you hope—that your misgivings can be addressed, that there are solutions, and that you can change. That's all.

Maybe if I tell you how I got here, you'll see where all this hope is coming from.

I met a child who could not walk. He could not sit up or hold up his head. He could not talk. His mother had brought him into my parents' shoe store for special corrective shoes. But to see his skin-on-bone arms and legs, you knew this child would never wear out these shoes; would not even outgrow them.

My usual customers were lively boys and girls who participated in the purchase: the parent would explain why a particular shoe was just perfect, the child would complain, the parent would urge, the child would insist, the parent would argue, "The white sandals would look pretty with the anklets grandma bought you, but the patent leather is better for your Sunday dress." The child would point and scowl ... but not the child in front of me. The mother had propped him up on the chair, handed me the prescription for the "surgical boots," then crossed her leg over to face away during the whole of the fitting. Not another word was spoken.

I was shaken by this encounter, but I learned something of ultimate importance to me: no matter what hand you are dealt by fate, if you cannot communicate, if you cannot speak, you are truly forever on the outside of life. I wanted my life to matter, and helping people to learn to communicate ... now *that* was worth life's labor. I went to college and ended in the graduate program in speech-language pathology at Northwestern University in Illinois. It was there that I learned that the child I just described was made flaccid by hypotonic cerebral palsy.

During my clinical practice as a speech pathologist, I found myself working with another young person with cerebral palsy at the hospital speech clinic. She was a teenage girl, somewhat developmentally delayed and severely spastic. She had difficulty keeping her mouth closed—something important in making certain speech sounds and in eating and looking OK. We had worked together for a number of weeks and had found how to position her wildly spastic body for the greatest degree of calm and control, how to get her jaw into alignment, and with tactile stimulation to the lips, how to help her to close her lips for as long as possible. This posture was like stacking a house of cards: you held your breath as she struggled to maintain the posture and control, feel her lips together, and breathe through her nose. This was the therapy goal.

And then some doctor would stride by, stopping to muss her hair and say in a jolly, jolly voice, "Christine, are you still my favorite girlfriend?" And Christine would lose all control and practically jerk out of her wheelchair with great flailing of all her limbs. The doctor would march away, clearly so pleased with himself.

And I was left enraged, furious with the doctor for his condescension, arrogance, and insensitivity. I was also furious with Christine's parents who dressed her as a little girl and gave her none of the grooming niceties of other teenage girls. How about a nice hairdo, folks? How about a dab of lipstick? Would it kill you to dress her like a young lady instead of a handicapped child? Oh, I was full of frustration, but my role as a speech pathologist would not allow me to do anything about this. My therapy goal was to help her close her mouth, so I had to close mine. I wanted to do so much more.

I had to wait for several years until I opened a private practice as a speech pathologist in a medical building associated with a hospital in San Francisco. Here I had a surprise. For every person with a stroke or a stutter who walked through my door, there was a doctor or a hospital staff member who had some kind of communication issue! (My being a "doctor" made it possible for the medical staff to take instruction from me!)

The hospital personnel opened my eyes to all the ways that people experience "communication problems." There would be a nurse who was intimidated to silence by physicians and physicians who were frozen with terror by professional presentations at national conferences; young doctors scared of old doctors; foreign born-personnel who could not make themselves understood. The communication of maturity and power, as displayed by the voice and by nonverbal means, was a frequent issue.

One young doctor in training stands out in my memory: he had *all* of these issues. Kim came from a culture that did not support assertiveness in young people, and he never had the advantage of any speech help in learning English—for him, it was catch-as-catch can. He had no friends or support community. He was doing his interning under the eagle eye of a stern taskmaster (referred to as a sadistic something else behind his back).

Kim was terrified, and since his family and church had invested everything they had in his education, failure was not an option.

I turned on the recorder and asked Kim what he thought of his speech, voice, language, and general communication concerns. I learned the baggage that he brought into the room with him, right or wrong, and formed a pretty good idea of personal insight and motivation. What he knew were the critical comments he had heard, and what he felt was despair. He was currently being defeated by the articulation demands of the word "irregularity."

I played the recording of our interview and asked him to reevaluate the speech-voice-language as he heard it on the tape and to compare that with his initial evaluation. From this I would know how accurately he could hear and describe what he heard, which is valuable in understanding his skill and in making a prognosis. Kim was not able to make a judgment about his speech adequacy, but he watched my face to see what judgments I might be making.

Then I asked him how he *wanted* his speech-voice-language to be described by others. We would establish our goals and priorities by the way he answered this question: but all Kim wanted was to be a good doctor and to talk like one.

Because Kim was so weighted down with his self-criticism and failings, I figured he did not need further detailing of his communication deficiencies. All our work together was always presented in the form of pursuing his goal of communicating as an effective doctor, not solving his many "problems."

We started with vocabulary lists of frequently used medical terms that needed to be understood clearly and set a goal of ten words a day. I recorded our list for his take-home practice and he would phone (or stop by) every day to practice. This approach helped Kim take a positive attitude: every speech practice was an opportunity to make himself a better doctor. For him, that was enough to ensure solid progress on the speech clarity goals.

My work with Kim established the evaluative format and approach I would use for the rest of my career.

These early cases showed me that in a private practice, I could now offer the kind of intervention and holistic treatment I could not offer in a clinical setting because we had a direct fee-for-service arrangement and medical insurance was not involved. I learned that these people from the general and "normal" public were handicapped in their career development and that they had nowhere else to go for help. This was memorably illustrated by a woman in the hospital typing pool who grabbed my sleeve one day and said, "Dr. Fleming, I once worked in an office and there was an opening for a manager;

I tried for it, but the boss said my voice was too airy-fairy for the promotion .... We didn't have people like you back then." I knew I was in the right place doing the right thing.

This work has led to unimagined personal rewards from people who taught me a thing or two about character and talent and determination. You will meet some of them in this book, but first let me tell you about Elaine, who will humble us all with her courage.

I learned from her phone call that Elaine wanted to pursue another job in human resources in Silicon Valley. She had previously headed HR in a major San Francisco company for twenty years, but the department was to be closed. Elaine had an appropriate PhD and was highly thought of at her present company, but she told me that the headhunter she was working with had let her know that her voice was probably "too soft" for this new young company she was considering. She asked for an appointment to work on her "soft voice." Between you and me, I was already suspicious about this voice complaint just by the way she spoke on the phone. But OK, an appointment was made.

The time came, and Elaine walked in the door. She was what? 4'10"? On the chubby side, clearly late middle-aged. She made no effort toward coiffure or makeup or accessories. Her long, flowing pant legs were an attempt to cover a bone-thin leg and the 6-inch platform of her big, black orthopedic shoe; she had had polio as a child. I immediately understood what "your voice is too soft" actually meant. A loose translation would probably be "this new company has young, smart, and with-it techies; they are the cutting-edge future and you ... aren't. You are dumpy, plain, old, chubby ... crippled." The headhunter solved her dilemma by saying Elaine's voice was "too soft."

She was off the hook, but I was on it. I admit I took a deep breath on this one, but, sensing her maturity, I leveled with Elaine about my suspicions, and she handled it like the pro she was. "Do you want to deal with this situation?" I asked, and she said, "If you think I can do it." I did.

Now I could do the makeover I couldn't do for Christine. A new hairdo, makeup consultation, amber jewelry to make her big brown eyes light up her face, a more fitted seafoam green outfit, and our secret plan. She told the recruiter that she had worked with a voice consultant and was now ready to try out for the job.

Applicants for the human resources leadership position were to present a twenty-minute talk on some aspect of that field. Elaine chose "diversity," and we went to work on her presentation. She knew her professional stuff, of course, but I offered an opening that I thought would command the kind of fresh respect she needed and switch their attention from her crippled leg to her strength of character. She was astonished at my plan but agreed to do whatever it would take. Here is the opening of her talk:

(Standing in front of the group, take your time and make eye contact til they've settled down.)

"How old were you when you first found that you were different from other children?"

(Long pause, let them think.)

"Well, I was 5 years old when I saw that they didn't look like this."

(Hike your pant leg up to your thigh and just stand there, making them look at your leg and shoe. Don't rush, make eye contact. Now, go on to your presentation.)

Elaine turned down this job offer to take a better one. She had learned that she didn't need to cover her leg in shame, something she had done all her life. She could truly put all her professional weight on that leg and march into her career with her head up.

And *I* learned I could not only help people speak better, I could help them *be* better.

They could present a more confident face to the world and have more trust in their own abilities; speak out about the concerns of others—and their own—more forcefully; be perceived as leaders in their companies and communities; participate in social gatherings with more comfort and fluency; feel that they are fulfilling their potential; speak their mind more effectively; and earn the respect of others.

It is my hope that this book will help you be better, too.

Carol Fleming
August 2, 2012
San Francisco

Introduction

As you communicate with people, they come to know you both as an individual and as a professional. The only way that people can sense your intelligence and professionalism is through the effectiveness of your communication: what they hear you say, the attitude that they perceive, and the very sound of your voice.

Professional communication is important to people in every line of work. While your expertise and skills are, of course, essential, it is your personal verbal communication that transmits your expertise and confidence to other people. While many books out there on communication will tell you what to say, few address how to say it, and even fewer will help you learn how to work specifically with your speech and your voice.

I've been working with people on refining the sound of their voices for over thirty years. As a speech and language pathologist, I use the education and skills developed for the clinic and apply them to the more subtle needs of the business and professional world. While others may offer public speaking training, speech therapy, or theater skills, I take a holistic approach, helping people address any concerns they may have about the impression they make by the way they communicate both verbally and nonverbally. The reason this approach succeeds is that body, words, and voice must ideally communicate the same thing at the same time for the speaker to come across as professional, trustworthy, and appealing.

I've found that virtually everyone has some aspect of their speech about which they feel insecure or on which others have commented. People come into my office feeling nervous, and they always ask, "Can I really change my voice?" The answer I offer them is, "You absolutely can—with instruction and practice." In this book, I've laid out all the most common communication complaints I've seen, along with the exercises that I've used successfully with thousands of clients over the years.

This is not as simple or as straightforward as it appears since we have a unique relationship with the sound of our own voice. We *are* the sound of our voice. Our speaking is our personality. Our internal thoughts and feelings are communicated to the rest of the world with our voice. You draw much of your understanding of other people from just the sound of their voice. Even though you may be more or less conscious of this process, the vocal information is being processed at a level that is deeply visceral and emotional. So you've got to figure that people are processing your voice in the same way.

I'd recommend that you go through Chapter 1 of this book first. It starts you on an assessment of specific problems or concerns. A more detailed analysis is possible using the approach presented in the Appendix. The results of your efforts will help you choose the issues you wish to address. Chapter 2 is a series of self-contained chapters on specific vocal challenges, and each includes effective vocal exercises tailored to that problem. Once you've addressed all the specific vocal problems, you'll be ready to move on to the rest of the book. Chapter 3 covers voice enhancement techniques that will help you refine your voice into one that people will want to listen to. Chapter 4 covers what to say with that newly refined voice of yours, and Chapter 5 will help you pair your verbal communications with appropriate and persuasive body language. Finally, Chapter 6 goes into how to adjust your communications for specific professional circumstances, including job interviews and presentations.

While every chapter in this book is self-contained, some readers may find that they'd like to hear examples of specific problems. My CD, *The Sound of Your Voice*, is available if you'd like to refer to that additional resource.

You might start looking for a recording device for your speech and voice work because listening to instructions, examples, and your own efforts is usually an important part of speech and voice change. In addition, you will need to be able to record, pause, play, and replay. Your recorder should have a counter so you know where you are. You want as high a quality as you can manage so you can hear yourself accurately.

Many of you might want to use miniature digital recorders for our work. If you are working on speech or voice, these devices may *not* be adequate. However, if the quality of sound is not an issue, such as when recording a passage for speed control, the smaller digital recorders might be useful.

There are action steps in virtually every chapter, because you will change your speaking by practicing a new behavior until it replaces the old, unwanted one. The qualities of perseverance and patience will be important to you.

One of my clients, a young woman from New Zealand, managed a credible American accent after only two lessons. Another client was a young, beginning newscaster. He brought me videotapes of his first assignments, and we both agreed they were embarrassing. We analyzed them for clarity and professionalism and made a makeover plan. In one week, he was a different person: mature, composed, and television-ready. I saw him on the newscast just last night. These two people were *highly* motivated. When you are completely committed to change, you will have the motive and strength to ignore distractions and maintain the practice schedule required for behavior change. I've never had one client regret the work that it took to achieve a new, more effective vocal communication style.

Some people have painful memories of failed attempts at self-improvement. From what I've been able to observe they have greatly underestimated the necessity of focused and sustained effort. They make a few gestures toward their goal, don't see immediate results, and conclude, "It doesn't work!" It does, too!! We know that there is nothing more important than *deliberate practice* in behavioral development. The word "deliberate" means that you must be mindful of the improvement you are trying to make. Your attention must be completely involved in learning. Your motivation will help you focus completely on your task. If you need any evidence on the efficacy of deliberate practice, take a look at Malcolm Gladwell's *Outliers: The Story of Success*. For those of you who want to examine the research that led up to the famous "ten-thousand-hour" formula, I have included the Ericssen reference in the Citations section. Do not think that you can practice successfully while the television is on, or while you are doing anything else. The roots of our communication patterns are too deeply embedded in our brains for superficial efforts to have any effect. I have seen the lives of business and professional people become increasingly pressed and pressured. They do not "have" the time to work on their speaking; they must "make" the time.

I usually ask people to practice at least three or four times a day for six- to twelve-minute practice periods. People frequently imagine that they are going to put in a good solid hour of practice right after dinner. They fool themselves. They will be tired and distracted at that time. An hour is too long for the kind of concentration it requires. But frequent, short practice periods work very well for the adult learner. You must find the schedule that allows you to devote your complete attention to your speech work. As much as you would like to use the apparent "downtime" of driving to practice, I urge you to resist the opportunity. Driving is far too dangerous an activity to complicate with speech learning.

Try to make it fun, and give yourself a reward for each day you complete your full practice time. Give the new learning a chance to become easy and habitual. If you've got the motivation for deliberate practice, you will get good results for your efforts.

One last tip before we get started: Any new behavior, speech or otherwise, will feel strange (wrong, weird, or phony). What feels fine is how you've always done it. What *feels* alarmingly strange will probably *sound* quite good. I promise, over time, the new habit will become the one that feels most comfortable. Remind yourself that this improvement will help you get to where you want to be in your career and in your life in general. It's good to ask a few trusted friends to listen to you and offer you regular feedback, but make sure everyone knows that virtually everyone who tries a new communication pattern does so in a stilted, overly correct manner because they're speaking self-consciously. This will smooth out, I promise. We are aiming for easy, natural-sounding speech, and that will come in time with deliberate practice.

Understand that you are setting your foot on a path that will have the greatest impact on your life and will be worth extraordinary commitment. The great Henry James had this to say about your journey:

> All life therefore comes back to the question of our speech, the medium through which we communicate with each other; for all life comes back to the question of our relations with each other ... the way we say a thing, or fail to say it, fail to learn to say it, has an importance in life that is impossible to overstate—a far-reaching importance, as the very hinge of the relation of man to man.

CHAPTER 1

Assessing Your Voice

If you ask people how they want their speech and voice to be described, they will probably say articulate, resonant, and knowledgeable, clear, persuasive, and confident. These are the characteristics of speakers you admire, and you want to be in that club because you know how very much it matters. As one of my clients said, "Every time you open your mouth, you put your business in the street" (i.e., you put your reputation on the line).

I will tell you a secret: People are not good judges of their own speaking characteristics. They may be aware that there's something about the way they talk that is a problem for them and they make guesses about the specifics. Here's what many clients say when they first come to see me:

"My voice is too high (too gravelly, too nasal, too ...)."

"I mumble/swallow my words, and I don't speak distinctly."

"I am very uncomfortable with small talk, public speaking, and interaction with any authority figures."

"My speech is too soft, and people are always telling me to speak up."

"I sound like a child."

"My voice is too feminine for a man."

"I'm terrified! I have to make a speech (deliver a eulogy, toast at a wedding, etc.)."

"I have an accent, and people keep asking me to repeat myself (or "people in the workplace seem to discriminate against me because of the way I speak")."

In this part of the book, we'll take a look at the assessment process. If you want to take a serious step in your own self-assessment, use the materials in the Appendix to help you get more objective feedback about the impression you make by the way you speak. The first step to improving is figuring out what specifically you'd like to improve so you can address the issue directly.

What Is a "Problem"?

A problem is some aspect of your speech that calls attention to itself or causes you or others to be distracted from your message. Many of the following chapters will describe features of speech that frequently cause problems. You will be told repeatedly to record and listen to yourself for the simple reason that you do not know how you sound; you only know what you intend. Trust me on this. Throughout this book you will find examples of persons who are shocked when they first hear their recorded speech, those who absolutely do not recognize the recorded voice as their own, and even people who cannot understand their own speech when listening to a previously recorded passage.

We have a unique internal relationship with our speech that is nothing like the waves of sound that other people hear as our voice. We hear our own voices right inside our heads, and this makes an enormous difference in the sound we perceive. Also, our brains are so involved in the formulation of meaning and language that we simply do not have the cognitive bandwidth to pay attention to how we sound.

Speaking concerns usually have two components: (1) aspects that represent linguistic learning, habits of speaking, and expression, and are amenable to change through specific identification and practice of new patterns, and (2) psychological aspects (tensions, anxieties, etc.) that can either cause or be the result of the speech pattern in question.

Let me illustrate this situation with Andrew's speech problem. Andrew, a man in his mid-twenties, knew there was something wrong with the way that he said the /s/ sound. When he was in junior high school, others kids would tease and imitate him, making a funny slushy sound for the /s/. ("I shee you're shitting on the sheet!") Oh, how very funny this was. And how humiliating to Andrew! You are probably asking where the school's speech therapist was. Apparently his problem was considered "too minor" for these overworked people.

He was currently a backroom employee in a financial institution, but he really wanted a promotion and an increase in his salary. The position available to him would require face-to-face customer contact and some management communications. You can be sure that Andrew had avoided any public speaking situation up to this point. He decided to give it one last try, and he found me.

When I tell you how easy it was to correct his /s/ problem you will just shake your head in wonderment. Probably in response to a dental problem in the front of his mouth in childhood, Andrew had learned to produce an /s/ sound through the side of his mouth, by his incisor teeth (a lateral lisp). Normally, the /s/ is made right behind your two front teeth with the tongue forming a narrow channel to shoot the air right behind the dental surface. His lateral lisp became habituated, and he used it for the following twenty years. It started as a physical problem to which he adapted through learning, which had huge psychological consequences for his expressive confidence, which in turn had a major impact on his career path.

In one session, I was able to show him how to produce a correct /s/. Of course, it felt totally foreign to him and required much practice, reassurance, and monitoring on the recorder to make him comfortable with the new articulation. Then we had to go through practice situations of increasing speed and complexity to get the new habit secure. Andrew was highly motivated and willing to do the focused practice to internalize the new /s/. Four sessions later, our last, he entered my office, sat down, and announced with a twinkling of his eyes, "I am sssitting on the ssseat!" We enjoyed a great shared laugh, and it was a sweet moment. Andrew got more than just a good /s/. He got the confidence to speak in front of people and to reach out for the promotion. So you can see, emotions and habits are equally involved in the communication process, and both must be addressed to go forward.

What happens in my office?

1. An appointment for an evaluation is made. A few people, like Andrew, know exactly what their problem is, but most people have to make wild guesses and need professional clarification in order to proceed. The evaluation takes about an hour. From your side of the desk, you are having a simple conversation about your inquiry, with some questioning about your background or relevant present-day situation. You soon forget that you have a microphone in your face!

Next, we will listen to that recording together to make a more realistic decision about the impression you make by the way you speak. You will NOT want to do this at first, but I will pretend that I don't know that and go right ahead. You soon get over your apprehension when you see that I am not going to beat up on you but will be trying to help you understand what you are hearing about yourself. Then you will love it. You may well be able to hear that you speak a lot better than you thought you did. In any event, you are confronting your "self" as never before. You will be surprised, and you will feel elated.

Next we discuss our impressions and set goals for your progress. I will give you a general idea as to how our work will proceed and may even get you started on some aspects of our work. You will walk down the hall with resolve and hope in your heart and a lot to think about.

2. The second visit is an important one for *me*. I will ask you what you got out of the evaluation and will find out what was important for you, what you forgot, and what you learned about yourself. I will also find out about the quality of your practice efforts. I need to learn how you learn. At this point I will be giving you written materials to work with, and we will be recording elements of your homework so you can be sure that you are doing the right thing. There, I said it! HOMEWORK. This is what you do outside my office with what I have taught you inside my office.

If we are working on speech or voice issues, I usually ask that you spend a half hour a day going over our work in short periods of time—five minutes, but a mindful, focused five minutes—repeatedly through the day. I will ask you to telephone me with one of these short practice sessions so I can be sure that you are on track. We will make an appointment for the following week.

3. There will be many illustrations of how people practice in this book and much discussion of practice in different situations. Enough said. Some issues require several months of weekly appointments; it just depends on how much you need to accomplish.

Read on to meet the people like you who have worked on their speech, or go to the Appendix to get started on your own concerns.

CHAPTER 2

Resolving **Specific** Problems

Focusing attention on specific issues *works*! A vague wish about a generalized outcome *doesn't*. In this section, I will give you steps to resolve specific problems. Select one communication goal that you are the most motivated to achieve. If there are more than one, you can always go back after you've made reasonable progress on your first goal.

Consider the feedback you've gotten from others. How does it match up with your own listening? Many people are quick to defend themselves against critical description by attacking the source. "Oh, he just says I'm too loud because he really doesn't want me in the office anyway!" I have seen people discredit some excellent feedback this way.

On the other hand, now that you've heard a recording of your own voice, some of your biggest problems may seem clear to you. It is not unusual to have a listener in my office who is flabbergasted by his or her own recorded speech. "Good heavens! I can't even understand me! That's what they've been trying to tell me!" I've heard this many times.

Here's an example of a puzzling phrase I heard just last week: "Ana dina wana." In this case, you can probably figure out that the person was saying, "And I didn't want to." That is exactly what the person was thinking, but it was not what came out of his mouth. He was finally able to understand his speech clarity problem.

Many people benefit from a face-to-face interaction in real time with a professional speech expert. For example, if you have difficulty pronouncing certain sounds clearly, you should consult a speech pathologist to guide you. This is not the kind of thing you can figure out yourself. Check your Yellow Pages, the Internet, or go to www.asha.org to find professional help in your area.

That said, many common vocal irregularities can be cleared up with some simple training and effort. Those are the kinds of problems this book covers. As you begin to try out some new patterns of behavior, here are a few things to keep in mind:

1. A new speech pattern will feel strange (wrong, weird, phony, etc.). If it doesn't feel somewhat strange at first, you're probably not doing anything new. Only your habit will feel "right."

2. People will frequently try a new pattern in a stilted, overly correct manner. Be patient. This will smooth out with repetition. You're just trying too hard.

3. There must be systematic repetition to achieve real change. A few swipes at a new behavior won't change you. Here is where many people get frustrated ("I tried it and it didn't work!" Does this sound like some dieters you know?) You need deliberate, mindful repetition to make the new learning easy and smooth for you. Give yourself several weeks to practice several times a day, every day. Take whatever time you need; people change at their own rate. Start any speech change slowly and simply. By "simply" I mean that you should concentrate on the smallest unit—a word perhaps—and not rattle off a whole paragraph for starters. That's too much to pay attention to. Pick up speed only after you are confident that you are doing the correct behavior. Speaking changes are not quick; slow and steady wins the race. Keep your practice periods short—six to twelve minutes of concentrated time. Don't choose times when you will be distracted. Most people think

that they are going to practice while driving. *No you are not!* Speech practice requires mindfulness and concentration on the new pattern. Driving requires attention and the ability to respond rapidly to events. These two activities do not mix.

4. Carryover into real communication requires effort. It is one thing to repeat a phrase perfectly during your practice period and quite another to do it while engaged in real communication. Conversations tend to bring out the old behavior.

Develop short and deliberate conversations that are designed to let you practice a particular pattern in a pretend casual communication with neutral ears (people you don't know—the lady at the counter in the deli, the clerk at the shoe store, customer support on the phone, etc.), so the pressure of relationship management doesn't distract you from putting your attention on your improvement goal. For example, perhaps you are working on the voiced /th/ (*the*, *they*, fa*th*er). You are going to ask a shoe salesperson, "Does *th*at shoe come in o*th*er colors?" Practice this several times before actually addressing the question to the clerk.

This practice using real people is actually crucial in your development. If you can't apply new techniques to strangers, you won't do so with colleagues and associates.

Were I actually working with you, I might take you on a walk around the block, dropping into various stores to find a way to practice with a stranger. Why don't you just carry this book and pretend I am with you?

Fast Talkers

The rate of your speech most likely feels just right to you. It fits your temperament and tends to reflect your sense of urgency. But a too rapid pace of speech production can result in many shortcuts in articulation, forcing other people to *work* to understand you. Do you suspect that your speaking rate is a problem or an irritant for people? Let's take the first step toward finding out!

The reading material below has easy, uncomplicated, and unemotional language. You are going to be reading this passage out loud. Practice this passage at your usual rate of speaking—this will take some doing. Get some feedback from a friend to see if you are successful at this. The very act of reading out loud tends to slow people down, so if you are too fast reading this material, you're too fast in conversation.

Practice Passage

(From *The Snake Has All the Lines*, Jean Kerr)

I never bring reading material aboard a plane because I am convinced that if I'm not right there, alert every minute, keeping my eye on things, heaven knows what might happen. When it comes to selecting a seat I am torn between the wish to sit well back in the tail (surely the safest place to be when we crash) and the feeling that it is my civic duty to take a place next to the window where I can keep a constant watch over the engines. You have no idea how heedless and selfish some passengers are—reading magazines and munching sandwiches all the while that I, alone, am keeping that plane aloft by tugging upward on the arms of my chair and concentrating intensely, sometimes for hours. And when it becomes absolutely clear that something is amiss, who has to ask that simple, straightforward question that will clarify things? I do. Honestly, I don't think these people care whether they live or die.

Now record the passage. You are going to listen to this tape and make two determinations:

1. How does it sound? Better yet, have someone else (your external ears) listen and tell you how it sounds. This other person is especially important because you are likely to "hear" what you *intended* to say, not what you *actually* said.

2. How much time did it take you? The passage below has about 160 words and ideally should take about one minute to produce. Anything between 155 and 175 wpm (words per minute) would be an excellent rate for normal conversation. This can serve as your target reading rate.

If you dashed this passage off in something like thirty seconds, you are speaking way too fast for ordinary ears. You need to speak slower. The more technical your material, the more you need to monitor your rate to allow your listeners adequate time to process your message, about 120 to 140 wpm. "More technical" is a relative judgment, of course. If it is new to them, slow it down. If it is old or predictable material, you can speed up. The more people to whom you are speaking (or the larger the room is in which you are speaking), the slower your speech should be. You need to adapt to the room acoustics and the age of your audience. Many older people have age-related hearing problems that require more processing time. The more distractions and noise that are present in the room, the more difficulty people will have in hearing what you have to say. Pay attention to the speech rates of other people—including radio and TV announcers—to bring it into your consciousness. Perhaps you are associating with many people (especially your family) who speak rapidly as part of a cultural style. This will have a strong influence on your own speech rate.

If you have found that you routinely speak too fast (through feedback or actual word count), you need a strategy to break your habit. Think of it as developing a separate way of speaking, like speaking another language or playing a part in a play. Consider this slower rate as another dialect available to you in addition to your *habitual* style. We know how to develop these new speaking habits.

- Read the practice passage until you can hold it to one minute. Record it. Listen to it several times to get familiar with the *feel* and the *sound* of this pace: the breathing rhythm and the timing of the articulation. Spend some time on this step so you can really learn how it feels in your body.

- Find other reading material that is an easy narrative or description, perhaps a newspaper article, and try to read it at the 160 wpm rate. Keep checking your wpm and your timing. *Warning*: you may start just fine but lose your focus and speed up as you get involved with your material. Watch for this. Effective practice must be mindful and deliberate, with your goal ever in your mind. This is especially true when dealing with rate control.

- Listen to this tape several times to build familiarity and comfort with the rate. Find different material and repeat the record/listen procedure.

- Imitate your recorded speech without reading. Think of something easy to talk about and say it out loud. You might start with a passage that you have memorized in the past, say the Gettysburg Address, to practice your rate control.

- Leave a recorded message for yourself on your own phone so you can listen to it later to hear if you actually use the slower speaking rate.

- Call your external ears and try to maintain the 160 wpm rate. Record, listen. Record, listen. Record, listen. You need to do enough of this purposeful practice to make this rate comfortable for you. Your success depends primarily on your willingness to practice deliberately.

- Use the rate with neutral listeners. These can be phone inquiries, questioning a store employee, or making a restaurant order. With enough practice here, you can start having success using this rate with the people that matter to you.

- When you feel yourself getting emotional, you will undoubtedly speed up to your old rate of speaking. Remind yourself to use your reading aloud rate. It will be like going into dialect: a better—more mature, authoritative, and articulate—dialect.

I Think Faster Than I Can Speak!

Some people explain their rapid speech as an attempt to accommodate the speed of their thinking. They must think that slow speakers are, therefore, slow thinkers. This is a common stereotype. In *Do You Speak American?* MacNeil and Cran quote an individual describing a Southern person's speech as "so slow it was like bubbles coming up through a swamp. I guess that must be the way his mind works." Let me assure you right now that such conclusions are unwarranted. The Southern dialect, by the way, is the largest dialect group in America and shows no signs of diminishing.

When people respond to a personal sense of urgency, they take some articulatory shortcuts: First, their articulation (the speech movements that make the idea transmitted to the listener) may be incomplete. And second, their intonation is stifled in this press for speed. This is in contrast to a speech rate that is more attuned to the hearing needs of the listeners. Pay attention to the chapter called "Speaking Your Mind Effectively" where we examine the difference between self-expression and communication. The latter always considers the receiver in the formulation as well as the articulation of the message. The former, well, doesn't. What makes this situation especially difficult is that the "too fast" speakers are not aware that their speech has become degraded and difficult to follow. Their sense of urgency overrides self-monitoring and the consideration of the needs of the listener.

Getting Aware of "Too Fast" Speech

When Fernando finally listened to what his colleagues and clients were trying to tell him—that he was speaking too darned fast for easy comprehension—he took responsibility and began his training with me. He *could hear* that it was a problem when he listened to our taped initial interview. The fast speaker really needs help in identifying *how it feels* to speak with such speed and urgency if he is going to have any chance to modify the rate. Like all speakers, he is focused on his intent and internal sense of meaning, not on the actual speech movements.

How We Started

I would engage Fernando in conversation and soon enough he would begin to break the speed limit on his clear speech and begin to slur his speech sounds. At this point he would hear me press a clicker to alert him. He had been instructed to stop speaking, consider his thought, look directly at me, and thoughtfully select his language. He needed to increase the frequency of pauses in his speech (with the help of Mr. Alligator, the clicker), wait for me to nod, signaling comprehension, before he continued. It drove him crazy, this pulling him out of his personal sense of expression into the discipline of considering the other person.

With Fernando it made sense to transcribe a paragraph of his spontaneous speech and examine what he was trying to say and how many words he used to say it. What we found were many repetitions and extraneous comments. We would reformulate the information to show how he could have given the actual content of his paragraph in just two sentences. This exercise became his daily homework: to record, transcribe, and reformulate in a tidier fashion. This reformulation was what had to happen in the pauses we were inducing with the clicker. In a short time, just the sight of the clicker made Fernando pause and consider his speech rate. It succeeded in getting his attention and raising his awareness of the listening and comprehension needs of other people.

Fernando insists that I scarred him for life and that he continues to have nightmares about Mr. Alligator. But he says this with a twinkle in his eye … and with much slower speech.

Loud Talkers

People listening to Karin frequently wish that she had a *volume* control knob that they could adjust. While her loudness level is usually appropriate in normal conversation, she has the capacity and tendency to get "amped up," as she calls it, during emotional exchanges, and then the whole office knows it. Her colleagues roll their eyes, close their doors, and avoid Karin. She sounds very scary, aggressive, and threatening. You'd think that Karin would know this, right? Wrong! Karin is oblivious and vociferous in denial.

"I don't think I'm too loud! I mean, it's only natural that you're going to get a bit upset when other people mess up all your work. Other people talk loud sometimes and they don't get criticized like this!"

Karin had marched into my office full of rage, having been sent to me by her office supervisor. A "too loud voice" was just one of her identified communication problems on her performance review.

The first job—though not the simplest job—was to get Karin to own the problem. The fact that her employment was at stake had certainly gotten her attention, but she was too hurt and confused by the criticism to be able to deal with the issue. I offered my observation that she seemed to have a wonderfully spirited personality and larger-than-life expressive characteristics, and I wouldn't be surprised if sometimes this came across as overwhelming to folks not as lively as her. Reframed and newly interpreted, she was now able to at least consider the loudness level of her speaking.

Because the judgment of volume is so subjective, I sometimes have to show (rather than tell) people what they're doing with an electronic device. A sound level meter can be purchased at a local electronic store. I place the instrument between my client and me, making sure that it is smack-dab in between us. I set the response range so that my speech volume level is in the middle of the response range. Clients can see the needle flickering mid-dial. When they speak they may see it swing over and clang at the upper limits of the volume indicator, the red zone. The VU meter on an audio recorder can give you much the same information. This is powerful objective feedback about relative loudness, much more convincing than someone's opinion.

Although Karin's speech was not always "too loud," I kept the meter available on my desk so Karin could see how frequently her volume hit the red zone.

If loud speech has been identified as a problem, your job will be to become aware of how it feels inside your body when you are loud. This "feeling"—physical and emotional—is your only independent cue that you are amping up. When you are feeling *this* way, you are probably sounding *that* way. You need to use this information to ratchet down your speaking to a more normal sound level. When the meter is not present, though, how will you know how you're doing?

If people sometimes step back to increase the distance between you and their ears, this just might be a cue that you are speaking too loudly. You can always ask them if you are too loud. However, be sure that you *never* get upset with them for saying so. They have to feel safe to give you this feedback or they'll stop doing it.

I sometimes ask my clients to talk to their supervisor (who probably referred them to me) to find a way to signal them when they are getting too loud in the work setting. They need to agree on a system. Sometimes I might stand at the back of the room during a presentation and give a discrete thumbs-up or thumbs-down as our agreed-upon signal of volume level adjustment. Karin's supervisor agreed to use this cue during meetings.

Whenever speech is markedly too soft or too loud, it is a good idea to make sure that your hearing is not impaired; get a check-up with an audiologist if there is any question.

Karin was pleased with her progress in controlling her loudness (so was her supervisor), but she stayed "larger than life" as a personality, of course. One day she was telling me how she told off her boyfriend. "I let him have it right in the old red zone!"

Soft Talkers

Tracy was earnest. Mark worked hard. But neither one of them could get their voice to carry to the last row of the conference room. Their speaking style was geared for the intimacy of face-to-face conversation, not for projection to a larger group.

People who cannot be heard will not be understood. People who cannot command a space with their voice cannot fully utilize their authority or knowledge. If people are always asking you to speak up or repeat yourself, you should learn how to increase your vocal power through *motivation, energy,* and *air support.* You access these resources with the following practice plan.

Motivation

If you are timid and unsure of yourself, your voice will certainly display your discomfort. You need to address this issue first.

Start by doing the up-front work that fosters performance comfort. For example, do proper research on your presentation and rehearse aloud (ultimately with real people, getting feedback on your content, organization, and general effectiveness). When you are confident that you're prepared, you are more likely to *want* to have your voice fill the space in front of you. *The lack of adequate preparation is the major reason a person will not demonstrate authority in speaking and will suffer from stage fright.* Please see "Speaking in Front of People" for more information on handling speech anxiety.

This attitudinal shift is an absolute requirement to move your agenda. This does not mean that you need to be Mr. Show Business to be a good speaker; you can be calm, centered, and genuine, but you can't give your words "gas" with your foot firmly on the brake.

Mark had put a lot of effort into a research paper for his professional association. But all of his effort went into getting it perfect on paper for publication. No time was spent on how to present it verbally to his colleagues. So he just read it quickly with his eyes glued to the page. He wanted the presentation to be over more than he wanted to be heard and understood. Sure, he *hoped* that would happen, but he did not *make* it happen. You make it happen by assuming command of the room and captivating the space with your voice. A reluctance to do this may well explain your small voice in the first place.

Written and spoken language are very different forms of communication. While we can read spoken language with ease, we usually do not speak written language well. Since Mark had always *read* his papers to groups, we first had to develop a sense of *conversation* with an audience. This was a new and astonishing concept for Mark. We worked in a fairly large room with Mark at the podium and me at the back of the room. And we would just talk to each other. I asked Mark to tell me about his work—whatever popped into his head—but to keep his face up and his speech projected out to me. I would frequently change my position in the room. We were getting Mark accustomed to (1) the amount of energy necessary to command a room and (2) maintaining eye contact with his audience. Please note that I am not teaching Mark anything new here; I am simply reminding him of what he already knows about making himself heard in these circumstances.

From there, we went on to a new way of speaking from abbreviated notes so he could not read his speech. He could glance at his brief topic cue words, but the content was to be discussed with his face open and available to the audience. He went from being a reader to being a speaker, and this made all the difference in his career and his personal sense of accomplishment.

Energy

As we have seen, Mark knew how to adjust the force of his voice for distance, just as you usually know when to whisper and when you need to shout. You can develop and refine this unconscious knowledge with actual practice projecting your voice across a room.

You can practice this at home. Place large pictures of people on the far side of the room. If you don't have any large family photos, you can find pictures in magazines—usually in advertisements—that will do the trick. Use photos that have the person looking right at you. Then speak to the pictures as if they were real people in the room with you. You will be practicing your eye contact as well as your projection if you focus on each face for five seconds as you speak, delivering a complete thought to each face before moving on to another face. Even if you feel foolish at first, don't quit! In order to learn something from this exercise, you need to keep it up until it becomes easy for you. Many have found that this exercise carries over to the actual presentation, and making eye contact (and speaking out at an appropriate volume) comes easier.

For best results, practice with real people—friends and family—so you can learn what your voice needs to do for them to hear you comfortably. These people will help you develop a sense of conversation as you speak to them, a fluency you want to take to your formal audience. When you are actually dealing with an audience, speak to the faces at the very back of the room. If they can hear you, everybody can hear you. Have your practice listeners let you know immediately if they are having any trouble hearing you by using a nonverbal cue, such as having an open hand visible when you are easy to hear and a lowered, closed hand indicating trouble hearing you. Please see the exercise for feedback in the chapter "Speaking in Front of People."

Air

Effective voice projection requires plenty of *air*, so you won't use throat tension instead.

Tracy wanted to become a trainer in the human resources department at a major oil company. Her lecture plans and visual aids were great; she had done that up-front work to create a presentation of which she was proud. She wanted to break out of the pack to be a leader. But she was all of five feet tall, one hundred pounds dripping wet, and shy in front of groups. You couldn't hear her unless you were within arm's reach.

When Tracy *tried* to speak louder, we found that she ran out of air rapidly; as a result, she was stopping to take in air at strange places in her stream of speech. Like many others, she had shallow breathing. Tracy thought she was breathing the best she could, and she assumed that she was just not built for greater air capacity. She was wrong.

When you hear a trained singer produce long beautiful tones that seem to spool out effortlessly and fill the hall, please know that that tone is the result of considerable preparation and effort, a good supply of air, and the confidence to use it. Speakers also learn how to maximize their intake and usage of air in order to have firm and clear voices. You don't want your body to carry too much tension that limits the expansion necessary for good air intake.

I look for signs of tension in the neck and upper thoracic area. I ask if the person frequently experiences pain and fatigue in the neck and shoulders. A positive answer means we need to start with some exercises that will help the individual identify the muscular tension and then contrast it with a relaxed state.

Stretching and Breathing Exercises

As you try this series of stretching and breathing exercises, go at your own rate and don't hurt yourself. Start with holding the stretch for five to ten seconds and work toward holding it for thirty seconds to allow the stretch to be more complete.

To reduce shoulder tension: Lift your left arm straight up close to the head and let the elbow bend so you are touching your spine as far down as possible. Reach your right arm low behind your back and try to touch or hold the fingers of your left hand. If you can't reach, you can hold a handkerchief in your left hand for your right hand to reach for. Hold until it becomes uncomfortable, and then switch arms and repeat the exercise. Your shoulders should feel warm and loose.

To maximize air intake without shoulder tension: After you've loosened your shoulders, you should feel a relaxation in the upper back and chest. Keeping that relaxed feeling, let your arms hang heavy from the shoulders. Take a deep breath of air into your belly, not into your upper chest. Imagine the air filling up your lower back. You are breathing down, not up. This will be contrary to all the images of "taking a nice deep breath" to which you have been exposed, where people heave their shoulders up and make a big deal of inhalation. Relaxed inhalation is quiet and rather invisible, unless you are looking at the midsection of the body.

To support breathing-friendly posture: Stand with both arms straight up in the air, hands bent back and flat as if you were pushing up on the ceiling. Put great effort into inducing tension into your arms and shoulders as you push up. Hold as long as you can, and then let go. Let your arms hang and relax; they should feel warm and light. Keep your chest up exactly where it was in the exercise, elevated and ready for efficient breathing. This is a posture you want to maintain throughout your presentation—chest up but shoulders relaxed. Notice that your respiratory movement is primarily in your belly or midsection. This is what we are after.

Now practice speaking to those pictures again, but consciously practice the relaxed belly breathing as you do so. Breathe in deeply before you speak; give yourself time to breathe fully before the next sentence begins. Continue this conscious, slowed-but-deep breathing as you practice your presentation. Pay as much attention to this deep breathing pattern as you do your words. You'll need to consciously counteract your old habit of grabbing for air in the upper body at first; with mindfulness and repetitions, this will become second nature.

Tracy's employer allowed her to practice in the very room where she needed to do her speaking. When you can rehearse in the setting in which you'll be working, you'll be much more comfortable during the actual presentation; it will be one less "new" element to adjust to.

Tracy found that she *could* muster up a larger voice for classroom teaching. At first she felt that her voice was too loud ("I feel like I'm shouting!"), but that was just because it was in fact louder than her habitual level. A buddy in the back of the room gave her positive feedback. In addition, listening to a recording of the presentation assured her that the level of projection was appropriate and effective.

Tracy had to work very hard for her achievement. Truth to tell, nobody in her department expected much from her (I learned later). She showed 'em.

Raspy Talkers

I have never forgotten Peter, a man who came to me because he felt his voice was really ineffective. And he was right. He was holding his voice back in his throat as if it were hiding as far away from human interaction as it could. This resulted not only in a gravelly voice but also in muffled articulation as well, not to mention a sore throat at the end of the day. Peter needed to learn to place his voice and articulation more forward. As a result of our work, he did manage this change because he was highly motivated to improve and threw himself into his practice with discipline and passion. I told him how impressed I was at how rapidly he had improved his voice usage. Let me share with you what he said to me after our last session:

> Prior to now I had been losing my battles with
> my boss because I felt my voice retracting and my
> attention was to my voice. The more I worried about
> it, the worse it became. And as I was worrying about
> how I sounded, I forgot what I was supposed to
> say. I would run out with my tail between my legs.
> But after two days of practice, when I met with him

yesterday, I felt very confident. I felt that I could
match him on a voice level. If I can be equal to him
on a voice level I feel I can be far superior on an
intellectual level.

After Peter left, I punched the air in triumph. Look at what
this change has meant to this man. And what a clear example
of the importance of your confidence in the sound of your
voice, the primary carrier of your meaning and your presence.
This one successful real-life experience for Peter formed the
basis of renewed self-respect. He sees himself differently now.
He knows how to overcome his raspy voice, not just in my office but where it really counts, in his interactions in the larger
world. This can happen for you as well.

There are two important aspects of the raspy voice that
need some thought:

1. The voice can be held back in the throat with
inadequate breath support because of sheer habit,
voice role models, or even a reluctance to speak
out.

2. The voice may have a raspy quality because of a
medical condition in the throat.

I highly recommend that you consult a doctor about your
particular situation, whether or not there is any pain involved.
In this chapter I have included a section on "Taking Care of
Your Voice" because vocal problems can ensue from just the
way we use (and abuse) our voices.

In the following discussion, I assume I am working with
a person who has a habitual voice pattern that is changeable
through learning. Sometimes people pick up a habit of speaking from their surroundings through an attempt to fit in,
especially in adolescence. It was, for Peter, just the way men
sounded in his Midwest hometown. Like all adolescents, he

wanted to sound like a man just as soon as he could. (We *all* want to sound like the people we admire!) When Peter heard his voice on our recording he recognized that he sounded just like his father.

There is a voice "placement" that is right for you, and it should involve the center of your oral structure—not high and in front of your face, nor back and low in your throat. But—just like Goldilocks found Momma Bear's porridge— "just right."

If you watch old movies, you may notice that the "bad guys" frequently speak with a clenched jaw and little movement of the lips. They are determined not to betray any emotion in their face as they speak—that would make them vulnerable. Try to notice the difference in those light-hearted or family films where people allow their faces to be mobile and expressive with speech articulation readily visible. Can you hear the difference in the intelligibility of their speech? "Bad guys" are harder to understand. Just as well, eh?

Kathryn wanted to be more articulate in her presentations to colleagues in her financial firm, both in person and in teleconferencing. People were asking her to repeat herself, and she was getting frustrated. She was trying to speak as clearly as she could. But as I listened to Kathryn, it was clear that it wasn't her speech production that was the problem; it was that she had a constantly raspy sound for a voice. It was a rough, hoarse sound, something like a creaking door. Her voice seemed stuck way back down in her throat with no possibilities of resonance or clarity of tone. I determined that the sound of her voice was not a matter of pathology but of habit, where she had become accustomed to making her vocal tone. Why do you suppose she developed this pattern? She was the first female in an office of very dominant men. What do you think?

I think she did everything she could to be "one of the boys" and to reduce as much of her femininity as possible. So she limited the amount of vocal variety of her intonations and pushed her average pitch level down to the bottom of her range. The sound she produced is called "glottal fry," a creaking-door kind of sound. Kathryn thought that this was the sound of her voice; she didn't know that she could produce a real vocal vibration that had a tonal quality something like the way your voice sounds when you sing. This is accomplished with a readjustment of the vocal cord tension and the air passing through the cords. I did the following exercises with Kathryn, and they might help you get started.

Exercises

Make the /m/ sound with your lips loose and comfortable, and hum for a bit. Do you feel the vibration on your lips? You will also feel vibration coming from your throat, but I want you to notice that there is also a vibration happening right up in the front of your mouth. That's where to focus your attention now as you open your lips and make the /e/ vowel, alternating the sounds (mmmmeeeemmmeeeemmmmeee) without taking a breath. Make the /e/ right up where you are making the /m/, as in the word "me." Make sure that the /e/ is coming out of your mouth and not your nose! (The /m/ has to come out your nose.) You may want to increase the amount of air you are using to produce your voice or even raise the pitch of your voice just a bit.

Record this practice and listen to see if your voice quality doesn't sound markedly smoother in this exercise. If it doesn't, you need to increase your air pressure to produce more of a singing tone without the rasp.

Use other vowels with the /m/, such as "ay," "uh," or "oh."

Try other consonants, such as /l/, /w/, or/ z/, remembering to keep the sense of the vowel right up in the front of your mouth and using the voiced consonants to help you place the sound right up in the front of your face.

Note: This exercise directly addresses the problem of starting your vowels with a sharp explosion of air in your throat at the beginning of syllable initiation. We are trying to avoid that by linking the beginning of the vowel with the voicing already present in the consonant.

Say the following sentence and put your attention on the contacts you make with your lips and tongue tip. Use these contacts as a focus for your voice: *Many members tried the pie.* If you put your hand on your throat, you should feel a constant vibration in your larynx. Now mark the following sentences for the consonant sounds that are right up in the front of your mouth. Hint: they are m, n, l, w, z, t, b, and p. [Caution: what is the speech sound that begins the word "one"?] It's the "w," isn't it? *My name is unusual. One alone to be my own. We'll meet whenever we want to. Leave me a memo.* Don't let your voice sink back in your throat; keep it up front with these consonants.

I had Kathryn bring me a copy of the material that she needed for her next presentation, and we used those sentences in our work, identifying the front placement sounds and getting her to place her voice up around those front consonants. Before she went into a teleconference, I would have her phone me with the first paragraph of her report so she could have some immediate and appropriate practice before the actual call (and I could check her consistency). I reminded her to think of her speech as proceeding from her lips right to the microphone to help keep her out of her throat.

Your habit will fight this effort, of course, and will try to keep you back in your throat. That feels natural to you. But you are trying to learn something new here, the feeling of vocal resonance up in the front of your face. I sometimes ask clients to phone their home or office phone number from my office and leave a short practice session on their own voice mail. In this case, I would stress the proximity of the lips to the mouthpiece of the phone to keep them out of their throat.

They can hear this proximity on the recording, and it helps them reconnect with the new speaking style and practice it correctly when they are not in my office. This is especially useful when you are trying something quite new to you.

The price for Kathryn's improvement was mindful, daily, and deliberate practice for several weeks, for she was truly dealing with a behavior that had both psychological and habitual elements to it. All I had to do to motivate Kathryn was to play her initial voice tape and she would shriek, "I hate it! I'll never talk that way again!" And she didn't. She has told me that she reminds herself to "kiss the mic" as a way of bringing her speech energy to the front of her face.

Taking Care of Your Voice

The raspy (hoarse, rough) voice is frequently associated with overworked or damaged vocal cords. If you are a professional voice user—and you are if your work depends on your talking—you need to learn some fundamental steps to preserve your voice.

Nowhere is this more important than with people whose work or avocation calls for extreme vocal effort. Coaches, drill instructors, and some singers and teachers fall into this category.

It is a good idea to form the habit of drinking plenty of water before you do a lot of speaking. The water you drink an hour or so before you speak will have been absorbed and distributed to the lining of your vocal mechanism (among other places) where it lubricates the surfaces and makes vocal cord vibration function well.

If you find yourself working hard to clear your throat, or if your voice gets sore and hard to produce, try increasing your water consumption an hour before your speak. The more you must use your voice for long periods (attention, teachers and singers) the more this is important.

Anything that makes you increase your vocal effort markedly or over a period of time can constitute vocal abuse and result in vocal rasp or discomfort as a first sign. Examine the source of your overworked voice:

> yelling at ball games, children, etc.
>
> excessive loud laughing or hard coughing
>
> talking loudly in noisy bars or around machinery
>
> just trying to make yourself heard over an extended period in a noisy restaurant.

"Lil Debbie the Dynamo" was a well-known fitness instructor, famous for her perky attitude; trim and muscled little body; cute, girly appearance, and low, raspy voice. The look of her and the sound of her voice were always in contrast. But if you observed Debbie at work, it would be evident to you why her voice was constantly gravelly.

Whenever she led a class in exercise, she exuded huge amounts of personal energy, demonstrating the physical activities the people in the class were to follow. She continued to shout out instructions, encouragements, and whoops of high energy to motivate her students as she led the class in aerobic exercises. Or she could be on her back leading the class in abdominal crunches, and she was still shouting, with her head twisted to the side. And of course, like most instructors, she had the accompanying music cranked up. So she was in full physical effort on her back, head twisted, outshouting loud music to forty people for an hour. And she did this several hours a day.

Let's see. Let's think really hard. What could possibly cause Debbie's voice to be chronically raspy?

I talked the management of the gym into letting me do a brown-bag presentation to the staff about the care of their voices when leading vigorous exercises, suggesting that they

- use amplification of their voice (if this is not an option, try to always face the class when giving instructions)
- turn the music volume down
- not yell so much (especially with their body distorted)
- omit unnecessary vocal noisemaking
- always face their class when giving instructions
- not talk and demonstrate at the same time
- be sure to drink more water

The Coach in the Boat

The coxswain of a competitive rowing club has to motivate rowers to overcome exhaustion, provide extremely precise and concise instructions on specific tactical maneuvers, and penetrate surrounding noise and clatter.

And the coxswain has to do all this with her voice. Casie, the sixteen-year-old coxswain of a rowing club, came to me *not* because she frequently "lost her voice" during midseason regattas (which she did!), but to have a competitive advantage in commanding her boat. Although most coxswains use a microphone or speaker system, there is still a heavy demand for vocal intensity. The head coach kept encouraging Casie to communicate stronger competitive emotion to the rowers. Casie would try by increasing vocal effort, specifically throat tension.

So how did I keep Casie competitive and still save her voice for another race?

First, I instructed Casie in "vocal rest." When she did not absolutely need to use her voice for competitive purposes she needed to just be quiet and let her vocal cords rest. (She already knew about drinking water.) She was to let her team understand her situation and find someone else to help give instructions and organize the team during preliminary setup activities, saving her effort for the competition.

When Casie got excited, she used mostly upper-chest effort in breathing, thus increasing the tension in her throat. She needed to develop greater abdominal breathing. If you look at the instructions for air management in the previous section, "Soft Talkers," you'll see the information Casie needed to redirect her breathing energy, out of her throat and into her midsection. We practiced this breathing approach using the actual commands that she would normally use in directing the crew.

Casie needed increased awareness of the level of her emotion during competition; she would put more pressure on her vocal cords to communicate urgency, and she had staccato releases of her voice (see "Staccato Talkers") when she issued commands. She started each syllable abruptly. We tried to visualize the actual competitive situation in my office as she practiced her commands, knowing that carryover to the real situation was the most tricky step in our work. Casie's situation was made much more difficult because the team coach focused on Casie as a motivator of the rowers. She insisted on hearing urgency in Casie's voice during races (which was the cause of the vocal abuse in the first place). After our work Casie was able to apply good vocal care habits, but only when the coach was not around! But her attempts did help preserve her voice, and her periods of discomfort were less severe and less frequent.

Sometimes people clearly have signs of vocal abuse, but there is no obvious source of overuse. It actually could be just the way they start a syllable in their regular speaking! Read the section "Staccato Talkers" to find yet another way to traumatize your voice.

Do I have to tell you about the effects of smoking on your vocal cords? I thought not. But I will share with you a notice

I saw on a lamppost in New York City twenty-six years ago: *Smoking is filthy and stupid, so stop it.* I did.

High Talkers

The number one concern of most speakers—male or female—has to do with the pitch level of their voice. They worry that their voice is too high. (Never have I been consulted by people who were afraid their pitch was too *low*.) But why this preoccupation with pitch level in the first place?

I think it has to do with the law of the jungle. The pitch of your voice depends upon the length of your vocal cords. These are two muscular folds inside your larynx (the "voice box" in your throat) that vibrate to produce your voice. Longer folds, which produce a lower-pitched voice, are usually found in bigger (more powerful) bodies.

This principle holds true for all kinds of creatures. Compare the roar of the mighty lion to the squeak of a smaller monkey. The sounds alone describe the predator-prey relationship. And, you will recall, big creatures eat little creatures with remarkable consistency.

In addition, the parental voice is lower in pitch than that of the (relatively small) offspring. The infantile higher voice is very effective in bringing out more tolerant and nurturing responses from the adult. You may have noticed that some grown-up people also make good use of this fact. Listen to some of your colleagues to hear if someone's voice sounds markedly higher than others and notice what your intuition tells you.

Perhaps you know the woman who looks forty and sounds fourteen? This youthful sound may well be a habit: daddy's little girl. When it works for her she can get the boss to either cut her some slack or increase his *or her* caretaking. It definitely diminishes the employee's gravitas. The manipulative aspect will be evident to colleagues and resented.

Since the lower-pitched voice so often describes the large animal as well as the adult animal, many of us try for the lowest possible voice we can muster. This is seldom a conscious choice, but you just may recall the circumstances of your first efforts to deepen your voice. It probably happened during puberty when you answered the phone, when you gave a speech, or when it was important to impress. The need to give off the radiance of the big, strong, mature person is acutely felt during that time, and forcing the voice down is something you can do to cope with the dreadful anxiety of this transitional period.

Here is one last story to make the case. It's nighttime in the bullfrog pond. The male frogs depend upon the sound of their croak to attract the females to them. The lady frogs prefer the lowest "voice" because it communicates that the fellow is large, thus more mature, successful, and desirable as a mate. Male frogs seem to know this, too, since the other male frogs will position themselves near the large frog and pick off ladies on their way to the big frog.

And it's not just frogs!

Hal was a prominent attorney sent to me by his ENT (ear, nose, and throat) doctor because of apparent vocal abuse. He presented with engorged, red vocal cords with a low-pitched, hoarse voice. Clearly a case of vocal abuse that was on its way to produce vocal cord nodules (small growths on the cords), said the physician. Hal's history revealed that he went to Israel frequently where he had lively arguments in close quarters. His associates smoked heavily and they shouted at each other a lot.

I experimented with his pitch level, raising it a bit to produce a clearer tone, and we practiced using that pitch level in our discussions. His voice was clearer and certainly more comfortable. I designed a practice program that had him using this voice outside my office. He looked at me with alarm. "What!? And give up my low, sexy voice?"

Note: You may know a man who rather enjoys his low, gravelly "Godfather" voice and image. Keep nudging him to have an ear, nose, and throat doctor take a look. There might be a condition that is best dealt with early.

And it's not just men!

I will tell you about Nicole, one of my failures. Her boss contacted me and told me that one of their top patent attorneys had a certain style that was ... well, it didn't jibe with her professional role.

Frequently this kind of description means that the individual in question comes from a working-class background and doesn't have the social polish, style, or even grammar of the other associates. "No, no, that's not it," he said. "It's too hard to describe. Maybe it's too feminine?" But if I could change her speaking style, they could use her with external clients and increase revenue, rather than just have her do the research work internally.

"So, okay, send her in."

Ms. Hotshot Patent Attorney turns out to be Ms. VaVaVoom—figure like an hourglass and dressed to show it off. Big eyes, nicely emphasized. Long, black hair brought up to the top of her head with ringlets falling down her face. And the shoes! Well, use your imagination.

I have made the point repeatedly that people are usually unaware of the impression they make by the way they express themselves. Not so in this case. Did I mention that she was French? Her voice was breathy, highly melodic, and, of course, French accented.

When I play the audiotape of our interview to my clients, I always ask the clients what they think of the sound of their voice. Nicole listened to her voice, smiled, and said, "Men think it's sexy."

Okay, what would she think of developing another style of speaking for the workplace?

"Why should I?"

Well, her boss thought it would be a good career move for her, expanding her contact with new clients.

Nicole shrugged.

Clearly Nicole had found a style of presentation that worked for her and had zero interest in accommodating her boss. No motivation, no change.

Is your voice really too high, or do you just *think* it is? It is not unusual to find that the individual really has issues with self-esteem and personal power or that he behaves in subordinate ways, elicits dominating behavior in others and thinks it was the pitch of his voice that was the operating factor. The classroom listening experiment that was described in "Hearing Yourself as Others Hear You" in the Appendix offers the best possible situation to make a determination of a high voice. There are exercises in the chapter "Getting It Pitch Perfect" if you think this is an area of concern for you.

I want to alert you to a pattern of pitch usage that is a bit tricky. It has to do with how to begin a sentence. Michelle had gotten the impression that her voice was too high, so she came to get her voice lowered. As I listened to Michelle talk, I noticed two things: in general, her pitch level was actually well within the normal range for women of her age, but I also heard that the first word in many of her sentences tended to be at a high pitch. This usage caught the ear and made the impression of a high voice because it was at the top of her range and she used it so often.

Try saying the following sentences as you think Michelle would: "*I* didn't say that. *He* was the one who mentioned it. *All* day I worried about it." Does it feel natural to you or really strange? Also, listen to the people around you to see if you can spot this pattern in others.

You must use your external ears to see if this information applies to you because you will not be aware of your normal intonation habits in any other way. Of course, Michelle was entirely unaware of this pattern. Once it was recorded and brought to her attention, she was horrified. Michelle and I got to work with some prepared sentences.

If you suspect that you may speak this way, try the following exercises.

Begin by looking at this sentence: "I would never do that." Pick a word (almost any word) to be a stressed word. This means it would be a little higher, a little louder, and maybe even a little longer than the other syllables. Let's say you pick "never," for example. You would have a pattern like this:

Start practicing your sentence at midrange so you can go up on the stressed syllable. Now do the sentence with the first syllable higher (this will take some surprising effort):

Then try shifting between the two versions of the sentence to experience your ability to control the stress pattern. Record and see what a huge contrast in meaning this little difference makes.

It will strike you as strange that I'm asking you to do this "problem" on purpose, but this is the only way that you are going to be able to recognize, control and eliminate the habit and gain conscious control of your speech intonation. You can apply this practice pattern to many different aspects of speech where you need to become mindful of the old pattern in order to replace it with the new. You must make the unconscious conscious. Got that? If you do it on purpose, you'll start noticing it when it just happens. You can't fix it unless you can hear it.

Because the sound of your voice is such a complicated issue, external advice can be particularly important to you:

- Consult a voice professional, like a speech pathologist, who is trained to make accurate observations and to give appropriate advice. You'll hear the objective information you need to make a sensible decision.
- Use the self-help CD (*The Sound of Your Voice*) mentioned in the back of the book. There are instructions to record yourself in a social context to get a much more accurate sense of your voice in a social setting.
- Pay attention to the consistent feedback you get from people whom you respect. If they say things like "You sound a lot younger than I expected" or "I heard your high little voice down the hall, so I knew you hadn't left," then you probably should look into this.

Feedback may come indirectly. The middle-aged woman answers the phone, and the caller asks to speak to her mother or the lady of the house. This is pretty good feedback that her voice may be too high, wouldn't you agree? If this happens to you, you are undoubtedly irritated and chagrined, but don't dismiss this valuable piece of information.

Caution: You may have a "telephone voice" when you answer the phone that is not really your usual voice. You may use a light lilting tone that sounds girlish. Or you may have a questioning, hesitant sound when you answer the phone with the voice trailing upward. "Hello? Who's calling?" This is useful information about your telephone habits, but it doesn't necessarily reflect your regular voice usage.

Many people find that they have worried needlessly about their vocal pitch. We do get some funny ideas in our heads sometimes! But these funny ideas can have serious and restricting consequences.

This chapter only considers the issue of "high" pitch because it appears to be such a common concern and because it is not at all a simple situation. The section called "Getting It Pitch Perfect" has practical exercises to actually work with other pitch issues.

Indecisive Talkers

Reid was notified in a written performance review that he had deficits in communication skills—specifically, that he lacked both authority and decisiveness. No examples, no clarification. Reid was surprised, hurt, and thoroughly puzzled. So he tried to act tougher. This ended in social disaster at work, and he felt like a jerk. Luckily, his was the kind of problem we could catch in an audio recording. Reid would make a statement of fact in a fairly flat tone. He would not drop his voice at the end of the statement; therefore it sounded equivocal, not definite.

Say, "I'm not going to put up with it," and keep your voice at just one pitch level. You will not sound very convincing. You will sound like Reid.

Reid needed to learn to create four levels of pitch in this sentence (and others like it):

The word "not" needed to have elevated pitch and would receive primary stress and "Up" would have secondary stress. "With it" would be said at a lower pitch than the rest of the sentence.

NOT

                  up

I am   going to put

                        with it.

Note: issues of emphasis and stress will be dealt with in the section "Getting Emphatic."

Reid started his work with a lot of simple repetition of this emphasis pattern. I would say other sentences with similar intonation, and he would attempt to repeat them. First I would tell him if he did, in fact, repeat them accurately. Then he had to develop his own feel for it. Later he would make the judgment himself by listening to the recording.

Reid was able and willing to imitate the patterns. This is not always the case. There are people, especially men, who are trying to talk at the very bottom of their pitch capability in order to achieve the lowest voice possible. Because they start at the bottom of their range they have no margin of their pitch range left to be able to go down in pitch to signal finality. In these kinds of cases, we first have to get the voice usage placed a bit higher in their natural range so that they *can* go down at the end of a statement. Trying to force your voice below the limits of your physical capability can result in severe voice abuse.

Auditory imitation is the fastest way to approach this issue. Some people are highly talented in imitating vocal patterns and are the ones who make the fastest progress. Do you have someone who can act as a model for you to imitate? I asked Reid to listen for the speech of an acquaintance that had a more authoritative speaking pattern that he admired. He was to pay attention to the melody of the person's speech and try to imitate it. (You will probably want to do this in private.) With practice, this imitation will become much easier. If you don't have an acquaintance or a colleague available to you, you can find your model on the radio or a TV show. This is good because you can play and replay to your heart's content as you analyze exactly what the person is doing with his voice.

At first, a new voice pattern will probably not be readily available to you when it comes to real communication with real people. You will revert to habit. Everybody does. That's why you need special practice to make these patterns more available to you for actual usage. It's called "carryover."

Write some imaginary scenes that make it possible to practice the sentence form. Pretend that someone has asked you a question. For example:

> Question: *Are you working today?*
> You: (speaking aloud) "I am not going in."

Example:

Try these sentences below. Remember that you need to stress one or more words to show meaning, but you need to come down at the end of the sentence to show finality. You may want to mark your written sentences for cues to go up or down with your voice if you find that helpful.

> Q: *Is Pete going to have to do your job?*
> You: He won't like that.
> Q: *Are you trying to bug him?*
> You: I wouldn't say it that way.
> Q: *Well then, what would you say?*
> You: I simply don't care if he has to do it.

Make up your own scenes. Practice. Record. Listen. Do it again. Make up other scenes.

Go down to the neighborhood drugstore and try to practice a conversation. You might think about what you are going to say first and try it out loud before you get there. "I tried this toothpaste. It claims to be for sensitive teeth. I'm hoping there is another flavor available." This is an intermediate step using the neutral ears on real people to expand your practice. Yes, I know you'll feel foolish, and, no, your practice partner will not be aware of what you are doing.

There are, of course, other cues in our speaking that contribute to the impression of indecisiveness. A pattern of offering softening phrases is certainly one of them that weaken the statement ("I was just wondering if ... if it's okay with you ... I don't know, but ..."), and you sound tentative. See "Using the Simple Declarative Sentence" for a more powerful form of expression.

Reid loved this work and developed a facility for the short, declarative sentence with the decisive intonation pattern. To gain both skill and confidence, we picked certain situations where he would make the effort to use this pattern, starting with neutral ears, of course. So he bought his toothpaste with real decisiveness. He ordered his cheeseburger like a captain of industry.

Reid belonged to a men's breakfast club and a local church congregation. Since the breakfast club began each meeting with personal introductions, we could use this weekly opportunity to practice his new vocal pattern in front of people who were acquainted with him. It worked well for our goals because it was a simple pattern that he could practice in advance and execute with comfort and success. His efforts at the church led to an opportunity to be a lay reader on the pulpit. While the King James Version of the Bible does not readily lend itself to easy speech work, we managed the archaic language of the weekly scripture by using the visual cues mentioned above to add vocal variety to the passages and to mark for emphasis and phrasing. He received much praise and satisfaction for his pulpit appearances.

Next on our list were his reports at staff meetings. At this point, Reid knew how to prepare his materials to manage a more definite speaking style. As he gained confidence from his repeated practice, he did not have to write in any more little arrows either.

Staccato Talkers

May worked in the counseling program of a university and had to speak to people practically every minute of the day. Sometimes she interviewed, sometimes she taught, and sometimes she consulted and counseled. Her voice was starting to feel tired and sore by the end of the day, so she went to an ENT physician. "Vocal abuse" was the diagnosis, she told me. This diagnosis frequently identifies people who misuse their voice by straining it when they talk, sing, or yell in such a way that the vocal cords get engorged, irritated, or develop small growths making the voice hoarse. May was really puzzled with this diagnosis; she had no history of yelling or talking loudly over long periods of time. Everybody in the department had to talk a lot, so it couldn't be that, she thought.

We found the cause in just the way she started her voice in most of her syllables. The sound was released abruptly with a kind of coughlike blast. This was the source of friction and irritation of the vocal folds. Have you ever imitated the sound of a machine gun? You probably used this hard vocal attack at the beginning of each syllable (aa-aa-aa-aa-aa).

Try saying the following sentence: "I asked Aunt Annie about our options." May would start each of the words with a little explosion in the onset of her voice. How about you? (This habit of explosive voice onset is called a "glottal attack," if you want to discuss it at cocktail parties.)

Say "honest" and "anger." Do you start them with an easy initiation of voice or a hard catch? Most people use a hard contact here, so we're using these examples just to help you feel and identify that hard catch in the throat.

Now try whispering the words in the sentence above, feeling the soft flow of air at the beginning of the words and the sentence.

Next add voice, staying alert for starting any syllable with the hard-edged opening of the vocal folds. You might try feeling the airflow with your hand before starting the voice. You will have more success if you keep your voice soft and the release slow; this will give you the chance to monitor and correct a habit of hard closure and release.

Make up your own list of words (beginning with vowels) that are useful to you for practice. Here is May's list: *actually, accounts, ever, every, often, HR, annual, invite, irritate, inquire, other, another, action, encourage, initial, evaluate, our, I, eager, over, only, on, an, in, any, over, up, ask,* and *entire.*

Say these words following another spoken word so you can just glide into the vowel with the air from the previous word. For example, "This_actually, those_accidents, when_ever, count_every." Let the air from the first word glide right into the vowel beginning the next word. This flow between words is called "linking" and is a very good thing indeed. No, it is not sloppy. It actually contributes to vocal support, clarity, and comfort in speaking.

Practice linking in sentences, marking the transition from the end of one word to the beginning of the next word that begins with a vowel. I have marked the following example from William James with a linking line between the words where you are most likely to put a glottal attack on the vowel: *Our lives_are like_islands_in the sea, or like trees_in the forest, which commingle their roots_in the darkness_underground.* It will help if you put your hand on your throat to monitor the continuous flow of your voice. Try this approach with other sentences of your own choosing. If you record it, I think you'll like what you hear.

You will probably glue your eyes to the paper on which your practice sentences are written. Put the material into your memory and lift your eyes from the written form. Or close your eyes as you do some repetition so you can deliberately concentrate on the auditory–vocal sensations. Finally, stand up and walk around as you practice, getting the new breathing and voicing behaviors into the whole of your body. Like all changes, this requires daily repetition and expansion to become your own. If you find that you use this staccato pattern, you should be on the lookout for situations where you are energized or angry. It is likely that you will really attack each syllable with maximum effort. Perhaps you should speak softly and carry a big stick instead. Hmmm?

May was able to use the linked, gentle syllables best in situations where she had a minute to think and compose herself. It was harder for her whenever people asked her to repeat what she had said or if she was trying to speak in front of a group. She told me that she no longer had any discomfort at the end of the day, however, and felt that she was more likely than not to apply the linking principle to her speaking, if you'd just give her a minute.

Breathy Talkers

When you allow air to escape with your voice and drop your pitch a tad, it becomes "soft"; this sound can be heard as intimate and sensual. Marilyn Monroe spoke that way. You will frequently hear an actress use this kind of voice when she wants to suggest personal intimacy.

Soft breathiness may be a matter of habit and quite unintentional. Because of its association with intimacy, a breathy woman may be heard as being "available" when that was not her intent. (But let's admit that some of you are skilled in turning this voice on when that is the signal you intend to send!) This breathy voice can be a problem for you and your listeners: It has low volume and is hard to hear especially in noisy conditions, it creates indistinct articulation, and you run short of air because it escapes in the tone.

If you suspect this may describe your speech, you need to use external ears to listen to you and let you know if they think this applies to you. As with most habits, the style of voice production will feel just fine to the user, so it takes an outside ear to identify the sound.

If you are wasting air, you will need to find a way to apply more energy to your voice production so that your air can be used more efficiently. Try the following ideas, and have your feedback in place to let you know what works for you.

To add more muscular tension to your vocal folds, just try speaking louder and see what happens. If this results in a clearer voice, practice using this amount of energy in a deliberate practice regimen. Let your external ears tell you that it sounds fine (although you may feel like you're shouting).

I have had a number of young Asian women tell me that their soft, breathy voices were encouraged in their homes and that "speaking up" was definitely frowned upon and considered unattractive. For many of these young women, what worked at home did not work in their place of business, and they had to face the conflict between the home and work demands.

When Kyoko walked in the door, I could read deference from her carriage and demeanor. Then she spoke with a soft and wispy voice so self-effacing that she practically disappeared. She worked for a major corporation during the day and went to her parent's home at night. She knew exactly what her problem was; she just didn't know what to do about it. Because she was so self-aware, I told her that she was "a smart cookie." This was a new expression for Kyoko, and she really liked it. She repeated it with a big smile: "Smart cookie!"

Kyoko was able to produce a strong, clear voice just from imitating of me, so learning a new pattern was not difficult for her. But what about the carryover into the workplace? That was the difficult part. A new strategy was called for.

We invented two characters for her that described the two dialects available to her. One was called "Kyoko," and that characterized her habitual voice and demeanor. And then there was "Smart Cookie," who walked and talked in a different way:

her body was upright, her gaze was direct, and her voice was firm. We practiced "dialect switching," using one style of speaking when it was appropriate and the other when that was the thing to do. The idea was to understand and respect the communication style of both cultures and to be able to use the appropriate style in the various settings.

I took short scenes from various plays and modified them so that one character was a Kyoko and one was a Smart Cookie. We read these scenes, taking turns being Kyoko or Smart Cookie (imitating the speaking style of each other) so she became facile in turning the dialects on and off. This was great fun for both of us. One day she gave me a written marketing report she was to give later that day, saying, "Read this in Kyoko!" Then she could laugh at me till it was her turn to read it in Smart Cookie.

This "dialect switching" worked very well for Kyoko because her social milieu at work enthusiastically supported the efforts she was making for clearer speaking. Though her parents knew Kyoko was smart, I don't think they knew about her being a Smart Cookie.

Kyoko was able to produce a firmer voice with only effort and modeling (imitating me), but sometimes the vocal muscles need a little reinforcement to make a firmer closure and resultant tone, so here is one exercise that just might help you.

Pick up a chair or something else rather heavy and hold it in front of you at arm's length. Talk for a while and see what happens to your voice as you do so. You may well find that the vocal folds come together more firmly and that your voice is clearer. Once you can get the feel of it you can try to replicate the sensation without using the chair. Again, ask your external ears if you are doing what you intend.

If the breathy quality seems to persist, please consult an ENT physician just to check that everything's okay. The sound of your voice could be an indication that something is preventing your vocal cords from coming together firmly, thus the escape of air. If that is the case, you should know about it as soon as possible. This medical visit is no big deal. It doesn't hurt, takes little time, and can provide much relief. Be a grown-up and go.

Fading Talkers

People had trouble hearing Owen when he tried to give reports to a committee at work. The beginnings of his sentences were fine. It was the ends of his sentences that seemed to just dribble down into mumbles. This created a huge problem when the whole point of the statement was in the last few words. For example,

> All of our efforts on the West Coast, beginning
> in January and extending into June, resulted in
> significant changes in the demand *for the product,*
> *leading to sales figures* of over 250,000 dollars ...

To the people on the committee, Owen appeared to just lose confidence when his words became difficult to follow during the course of the sentence. This is the most common interpretation of the habitual pattern of "fading," and this is why Owen's boss suggested that he work with me "to develop his confidence."

But sometimes individuals just don't manage their air supply during speech and run out before they're done talking. There is usually a pretty good connection between the thoughts we want to express and the amount of air that we take in to support the speech. This smooth working relationship between our thinking and our breath supply can become uncoordinated when our personal language process is under stress (for example, we are dealing with language suited for reading rather than speaking); we are operating with more sophisticated or complicated language than our norm—just using somebody else's language can throw us off; or we are in a stressful public speaking situation and our attention is fragmented.

Fading occurs when we continue to talk after our air reserves have given out and our natural ability to find a place to breathe is not operating. With Owen, we started by familiarizing him with the phrasal structure of verbal communication and the knowledge that just because words continue to appear on a page doesn't mean that he needs to continue to talk nonstop.

Spoken vs. Written Language

There is a great deal of difference between our language as it is spoken and as it is written, and this causes no end of difficulty for some people when reading aloud. It appears that their allegiance to the written form—sentences, words, and letters—is far more compelling than their confidence with the spoken elements—phrases, syllables, vowels, and consonants. Phrasing is a grouping of words involved in the same idea and is an important element of *spoken* language, which preceded written language by a long shot. But we are so heavily schooled in the written form that we have lost confidence in our ability to read aloud in a way that respects our natural ability to use phrases.

You should listen to how often other people pause, take a quick breath, and go on with their sentence. (This is not that easy. You are accustomed to listening to *what* people say and not the behavioral details of *how* they say it.) You'll see how normal and easy the quick breath is. Try to imitate someone who seems to have good control of their phrasing and air supply. Be especially mindful of the ease of hearing the words at the end of their sentences.

Find some written material that you would like to work with. It could be job-related or recreational. The very first thing you need to do is to recognize the phrasal structure because that's where we usually take a breath. Owen came up with the following example from work: *I have been reading all the reports coming from that department/ even those from the outlying branches/ and it seems to me that the situation is stagnant/ that we're on some kind of plateau.* The / marks indicate that a quick breath is appropriate and useful at this point.

As you examine each sentence of your material, see if there aren't units of meaning (phrases) that you can identify and mark. Now read the material out loud, taking small quick breaths between phrases. If you record yourself you should hear that your voice remains strong throughout the whole phrase. This is good. In addition, you do not want to hear yourself taking a big long breath.

Continue to practice this, limiting yourself to no more than fifteen words per phrase. The idea is to get familiar with pausing according to meaning. Practice for however long it takes to get this knowledge. If you are a parent with small children, reading to them provides an excellent opportunity for your breath control practice since the sentences are not complex. Reid brought in his children's books. He would mark with a pencil where he thought he should take a breath. He'd read, we'd record, and he'd listen till he was satisfied with his delivery.

Now lift your eyes and try a sentence from memory. If you record yourself during this activity, you'll be in a position to know if you've actually done what you intended to do. *The Night Before Christmas* is an excellent poem on which to practice this more deliberate phrasing, and you may already know this one by heart.

Here is a bit of excellent language that depends upon appropriate phrasing for its impact. You are going to break up the sentence into its component ideas. I am removing punctuation to encourage you to think about the sound of the material without the graphic cues. In the example below, it should feel natural to you to say the opening words,

"Four-score-and-seven-years-ago," as a phrase. At the end of the phrase is where you can grab a quick breath. Drawing upon your own sense of meaning, put in a slash (/) in the material below where you think a breath should occur. Use a double slash (//) for a longer pause for emphasis. (I'll put my version on the next page.) Read this aloud, record, and listen to find if you have clearly articulated all of Mr. Lincoln's words, especially those at the end of a phrase. You will find that this attention to phrasing will be the answer to a lot of your "fading" problems.

Four score and seven years ago our fathers brought forth on this continent a new nation conceived in liberty and dedicated to the proposition that all men are created equal now we are engaged in a great civil war testing whether that nation or any nation so conceived and so dedicated can long endure we are met on a great battle-field of that war we have come to dedicate a portion of that field as a final resting place for those who here gave their lives that that nation might live it is altogether fitting and proper that we should do this but in a larger sense we cannot dedicate we cannot consecrate we cannot hallow this ground the brave men living and dead who struggled here have consecrated it far above our poor power to add or detract the world will little note nor long remember what we say here but it can never forget what they did here it is for us the living rather to be dedicated here to the unfinished work which they who fought here have thus far so nobly advanced it is rather for us to be here dedicated to the great task remaining before us that from these honored dead we take increased devotion to that cause for which they gave the last full measure of devotion that we here highly resolve that these dead shall not have died in vain that this nation

under God shall have a new birth of freedom and
that government of the people by the people for the
people shall not perish from the earth.

Concentrate on the ends of the phrases to be sure they are
adequately supported. The rest of the sentence will take care
of itself. Imagine that you are sending out that final word and
the period at the end with energy. You may have a friend who
can discretely signal you if your voice is starting to fade away
during a presentation. Reid needed this kind of reminder,
especially toward the beginning of our work until he got the
hang of it. Reid's boss has congratulated us on Reid's improvement of "confidence." I guess it's not obvious that he deserves
the praise for *breath support*. But that's our little secret.

If I were I sitting beside you, I would probably mark the
Lincoln passage this way, but I might do it differently tomorrow. I may look at it with a different sense of interpretation
that would be reflected in my phrasing.

Four score and seven years ago / our fathers brought
forth on this continent / a new nation / conceived
in Liberty / and dedicated to the proposition that
all men are created equal. // Now we are engaged
in a great civil war / testing whether that nation /
or any nation so conceived and so dedicated can
long endure. // We are met on a great battle-field of
that war. // We have come to dedicate a portion of
that field as a final resting place for those who here
gave their lives / that that nation might live. // It is
altogether fitting and proper that we should do this.
// But / in a larger sense / we cannot dedicate / we
cannot consecrate / we cannot hallow this ground.
// The brave men / living and dead who struggled
here / have consecrated it far above our poor power
to add or detract. // The world will little note / nor

long remember what we say here / but it can never forget what they did here. // It is for us the living / rather / to be dedicated here to the unfinished work / which they who fought here / have thus far so nobly advanced. // It is rather for us to be here dedicated to the great task remaining before us // that from these honored dead we take increased devotion / to that cause for which they gave the last full measure of devotion // that we here highly resolve that these dead shall not have died in vain // that this nation / under God / shall have a new birth of freedom // and that government of the people / by the people / for the people / shall not perish from the earth.

CHAPTER 3

Developing a
Dynamic Voice

People easily make the leap from the sound of your voice to the nature of your personality. If you *sound* a certain way, you *are* a certain way. For example, "He always sounds so friendly." Have you noticed how good we usually are in making these judgments? Have you ever wondered how this happens?

A good speaking voice offers variation in the stream of sound. This is the feature that communicates your personality. These variations reinforce meaning and increase the intelligibility of your speech. The amount of change you produce in your speaking appears to reflect the extent of your emotional involvement. The sound of your voice carries your attitudes about what you're saying and about the persons to whom you are speaking.

Doesn't this strike you as an amazing capability?

I'll bet you have known people who use very little dynamic variation in their speaking. You're thinking about a particular person right now, aren't you? Perhaps your tenth-grade history teacher comes to mind. You may have used the word "monotonous" if not "deadly" to describe him. This was also the kind of voice you would produce when you wanted to portray the robot or the alien from outer space (take-me-to-your-leader) because it is an inhuman kind of sound, isn't it?

It wasn't just a matter of the speech sounding dull. The stream of speech was actually difficult to understand because you could not discern the stress patterns in the longer words, nor could you be sure which were the more important words in the sentences so that the correct meaning was conveyed. To illustrate how important vocal variation is to meaning, I'm offering the following (apparently bizarre) sentence, but I'm going to omit the punctuation that would give you hints about intonation. It looks like this: *John where Charles had had had had had had had had had had the teacher's approval.* Clearly this is a baffling string of words until given its meaning shape through *vocal dynamics* (and punctuation). It would also help if you knew the context surrounding the use of the sentence. But see if you can figure out the vocal pattern. I'll give you my version at the end of this section.

Do you frequently have trouble being heard in noisy circumstances? Lack of adequate vocal variety may be your problem. The male voice especially can become just part of the general thrum of human noise (traffic, restaurant, machines, etc.) unless a definite pattern of vocal sound is made available. The following chapters will give you more specific information about this aspect of your voice.

But let's step back for a moment and consider this amazing voice of yours as just one element of total expressiveness. To what extent do you allow your body to express variation in feeling, attitude, or enthusiasm? What about your experience with music, singing, and dancing, and in drama? If you are shaking your head no, it may well be that your personal style is to hold yourself like a closed fist, take no emotional chances, and remain as hidden as possible. In this case, your monotone voice is just one aspect of inexpressiveness. To express, to make your emotions evident, is to be vulnerable and that may not feel at all good to you.

To start, it may be helpful to consider other activities that help the body become more expressive (more energized and capable of change) without the emotional burden of direct communication with another person.

I frequently urge people to enlarge their musical/dramatic activities as part of a total approach to increased expressiveness. I stress the physical involvement aspect because speech and voice are physical activities. Physical expressiveness is something that comes naturally to many, but it is a new and dangerous idea to others.

Consider trying one of the following activities that might seem enjoyable to you. If you could fit in even more than one activity, that would be terrific!

Drama

Getting out of yourself and into another persona through role-playing seems to help many people use a degree of expressiveness not usually available to them. I have heard of famous actors that were reputed to be very dull fellows indeed until they assumed a role, and I have certainly seen this in my own office. I frequently use play-reading to encourage role-taking and expressiveness.

Phillip was in the financial industry and was very much the suited-up and buttoned-down type of person. He had had the experience of hearing a recording of himself giving a report on a teleconference and became aware that his oral reports were a flat drone. We started working with monologues from drama scene collections (available at bookstores) where Phillip could "be" some other person. When he assumed a role in a scene, Phillip showed he could be very expressive with variations in his pitch, rate, and volume. He didn't need to learn anything new; he just had to access a behavior that came naturally to him in other circumstances. He told me how very strange it felt to try out a new way of speaking. We recorded it, of course, for Phillip to hear that what felt funny actually sounded very good. When he had had enough practice with this form, we were able to transfer the expressive style to more business-type materials.

The most important part of his carryover work was to practice with other people present—family or friends—to keep the liveliness in front of others. As you might guess, the psychological pressure of the presence of other people tended to bring out his drone.

Children sometimes provide the perfect audience for someone like Phil to practice his oral expressiveness through the reading of children's stories. Most people know how fairy tales and the like are "supposed" to sound, using dramatic and exaggerated vocal effects. You can hear (and record) this greater vocal variety in order to increase awareness of this new melodic line. Phil used his nieces as one of his initial audiences for practice.

To really get outside of yourself, nothing beats improv. Improvisation workshops are available in many cities. Skilled leaders guide people through activities that help them overcome self-imposed boundaries of expression and discover the fun of spontaneity. It can feel like you have met a part of yourself last seen in childhood.

Dancing

If you're not a dancer, you should be. Learning to move with music, working with a partner, and getting confidence through movement patterns are all worthwhile steps toward expressiveness. From waltz to salsa, it's all good. And don't overlook the folk-dancing opportunities that are frequently available in the community. Circle and line dancing do not require partners and usually have many simple and repetitive steps that are comfortable for the beginning dancer.

You can also start by just watching dance. Look for the subtleties of movement in face and gesture that tell you about their feeling. TV programs such as *So You Think You Can Dance* demonstrate a wide variety of dance movements and styles. From casual to formal, slow or fast, there are many ways we move the body to be expressive.

Parents: start your children to move with music when they are small. Dance with them, buy them tambourines and slide whistles and form a marching parade, clap along with a recording, imitate the way different animals walk ... oh, the list can go on. Just get those little bodies moving and grooving.

Singing

Of course singing is the closest thing there is to expressive speaking. Singing has more tonal support and continuity of the voice but it involves the same use of change in the pitch, volume, and rate of the voice. Do I hear you saying that you can't sing? That doesn't end the conversation with me; it starts it. Let me tell you about Ivan.

Ivan had been called into the music teacher's room for a test when he was a boy. He was to stand with his back to the piano while the teacher struck a note. He was supposed to turn to the piano and strike the same note. Of course he couldn't, and he was sent from the room. From this he concluded that it was a singing test, and he had failed.

This happened in the Soviet educational system. They were probably searching for students with perfect pitch or tonal memory to select for advanced study. All Ivan knew was that he shouldn't even try to sing. There are many Ivans out there.

People with limited vocal inflection frequently tell me, "I can't carry a tune in a bucket" or "I had a teacher who asked me to stay in the back row of the class and not sing." Like Ivan, you may have speculated that this is the reason you have a flat, monotonous speaking style.

Each of the following sections offers a way to better understand and develop an aspect of vocal vitality as you move away from solving specific vocal problems and allow yourself to develop a dynamic voice that will deliver you and others a great deal of enjoyment.

Now, for that pesky sentence you considered earlier. Here's the context you need. Imagine an English teacher giving her students (John and Charles) the following test sentence. They were to pick the appropriate verb form: *Mary couldn't remember much about her visit because she (had had/ had) a cold at that time.* With this contextual information, try reading our sentence aloud with the vocal cues supplied by punctuation. "John, where Charles had had 'had,' had had 'had had'; 'had had' had had the teacher's approval."

Isn't it interesting how much meaning is dependent on context and on vocal dynamics?

Expressing Vocal Variety

Scientists have done experiments with vocal variety, such as putting earphones on people and playing four different voices into their headsets simultaneously. The person is asked to follow one of the speakers and write down what the speaker says. The listeners always pick the speaker with the most vocal variety in their speaking. It is simply easier to follow. The closer you are to a drone (monotone), the more likely you will be tuned out.

Even little babies and big dogs can interpret a person's mood by his or her vocal intonations. You can tell both baby and dog dreadful things but in a nice voice, and they will respond with delight. Speak words of love but in a mean tone, and you will get the opposite effect. Vocal dynamics are the variations in your speaking that carry the information about your own emotional and physiological responses to your thoughts. So it's a matter of the speed of speaking, vocal cord tensions, and forcefulness of the air. When people withhold this information, we get uncomfortable. Indeed, an important function of the voice is to indicate the way verbal statements are to be interpreted.

Rate refers to the speed of our speaking. Sometimes it is appropriate to speak rapidly or, on the other hand, to speak slowly and deliberately. We also need to consider pausing as an important element of rate. Do you? Pause? Ever? Do not underestimate the power of the pause in the context of a conversation or a speech. The pause allows the other person to think about or resonate to your message and achieves an understanding and intimacy that a barrage of words can never duplicate. (Public speakers: please note! The cultivation of the pause may be the most effective change you can make to be a better speaker.)

The average *pitch* level that you use is a fairly solid indication of your age, sex, and size. How your voice fluctuates in pitch—how high or how low you allow your voice to fluctuate—is a major determinant of how lively and melodic you sound. The infamous monotone means you pretty much stay near one pitch level when you talk. We'll be talking a lot more about pitch later in "Getting It Pitch Perfect."

You might ask yourself and others, "How easy is it to hear me most of the time?" Do you get the impression that your voice is markedly softer than others', or the contrary, that you're outshouting them? Ideally, one hears a mix of *loudness* levels. There is a time for added volume in your speech, as it reveals emotion (usually involuntary) or for the softly spoken word, even the whisper, to add an element of drama or intimacy. People can be monotonous with the rate and loudness of their voice as well as with their pitch.

How about you? Listen to a recording of yourself and focus on variation (or lack thereof) in terms of rate, pitch, and volume. Try to focus on just one of these features at a time. Remember, pay no attention to *what* you are saying; just listen to *how* you are saying it. Take your time to listen across a number of sentences before you make a judgment.

A musical voice is usually highly desirable. You have an advantage the minute you open your mouth. As I mentioned previously, people usually use a lot more vocal variety when they read stories to children than when they just speak with other people in their normal interactions. I frequently use this technique to acquaint them with their own ability to be more melodic.

Read stories to the small children that may be available to you in your family or neighborhood. Consciously try to add drama and emotional information into your reading to make it more appealing to the little ones. *The Oxford Book of Modern Fairy Tales* or *Mother Goose* offer some high drama and are perfect for this. A children's librarian will be able to offer a lot of advice and resources.

You might practice and record yourself to see if you sound involved and interesting or not. (The child's response will help answer that question, too!) If this is difficult for you, you might look for recordings of such stories in the library or bookstores and imitate the style that you hear. Pay attention to the amount of energy and interest that a real storyteller brings to the material. Imitate. Record. Listen. Try again.

I might record a story myself and send the recording home for you to listen to and imitate. If you have a friend or family member who is a great storyteller, you might ask them to record a good model for you to work with.

Once you have achieved some degree of comfort in changing your voice pattern, you can start using this enhanced range while speaking on other topics. Then it's practice, record, listen, practice ...

Identify a person whose voice seems to you to be melodic and dynamic. (Audrey Hepburn is one famous example of someone with delightful vocal variety.) This should be someone easily accessible to you to serve as a voice model. Try doing your best imitation of that person (in the privacy of your shower stall or wherever you feel comfortable). Doing so may reveal a capacity for dynamic change that can be developed. Record these efforts to hear how you're doing. "Before" and "after" recordings are very encouraging. You will need this encouragement since change, even positive change, can feel overwhelming at times.

You may be asking, "But wouldn't that be phony? Me trying to sound like someone else?" Would it be phony to be inspired by someone else's golf swing or hairstyle? We bounce off each other all the time. Whatever we can bring forth from within ourselves is ours.

If you think of yourself as singing while you speak, your vocal flow will be more flexible and your vocal tone will have excellent support. Singing by definition calls for pitch, timing, and volume changes, and should enhance your speaking efforts.

Perhaps the scariest part of developing vocal variety is that it forces you to leave the safe haven of restricted emotional availability (where nobody can find you) into the free air of open, accessible self-expression. Never fear—making yourself more open and available will attract others to you, and that can only improve your professional and personal life.

The Singsong Voice

This term is used to identify an intonation pattern that is stereotyped and repeated often enough to call attention to itself. It can be wearisome and childlike. A repeating pattern might sound something like this:

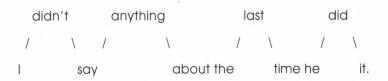

By itself, there is nothing wrong with this particular statement. But when the flow of sentences reveals a regular usage of the same pattern, it is a problem.

It proved to be a barrier for Joan, who was trying to get into news casting at a radio station. She spoke perfectly fine in her spontaneous speech, but when she read written material, out came her singsong (you *know* she is reading just by the sound of it) rather than the sound of a mature person speaking. You will recall the problem many people experience dealing with the written versus spoken language contrast mentioned earlier.

Her supervisor pointed out that she sounded childish, but neither Joan nor her supervisor could figure out exactly what she was doing to make this impression. So Joan pushed her voice to be as low as possible, thereby producing a muffled, strained sound that didn't work at all. She and her supervisor agreed that this was not working, and this resulted in a baffled but motivated Joan in my office.

We used both her ears and her eyes to work on her voice:

> *Auditory approach:* I would record sentences on Joan's practice recording using different intonation patterns, and Joan would imitate my sentence patterns. She was to listen to her tape repeatedly, continually improving her repetitions to match my intonation patterns.

> *Visual approach:* We would take a sample news item and mark the desired intonation patterns on the paper: when she was to make a phrase, when to pause, when to move her voice up or down, etc.

What worked? Both, one after the other. When she was able to imitate the recorded pattern independently, we could then use the written approach to remind her of how she wanted to intone the sentence.

Anything else? Yes, we invented a character for Joan called "Susy-Q," who read newscasts in an extremely singsong manner (negative practice). Joan would read the news in this style from time to time to heighten her awareness of her old habit. Then she could catch herself when it slipped out and correct it.

If you suspect that you may have the singsong pattern, you can ask a really good friend to imitate the way you speak. I would check with several people. Reassure them that this is really helpful information for your communication skills development and forgive them their exaggerated imitations. It's amazing what you can hear in other people that you cannot hear in yourself.

If this approach makes you ill at ease, a professional consultation can get you headed in the right direction, comfortably and confidentially.

Getting Emphatic

You will have noticed that some syllables in the flow of speech are more energized, louder than other syllables. This is a natural characteristic of human speech and an important element of *meaning*. The function of vocal emphasis is to clarify the sense of what is said. Some of these emphasized syllables signal word meaning and others indicate emotional meaning.

See what you notice about the following sentences. Read them aloud:

> He used his farm to *produce produce*.
>
> It was time to *present* the *present*.
>
> When are you going to *record* the *record*?

You pronounced the underlined words differently even though they looked identical. Aren't you clever! How did you know how to do that? I'll bet you didn't even stop to think, "Hmmm, in the verb form I'll stress the second syllable, but in the noun form, I should stress the first syllable." Right? Right!

This example simply makes the point that syllabic emphasis is integral to word meaning. It also illustrates that your knowledge of how to do this comes from subconscious learning.

Foreign-born men and women may use the vocabulary and syntax of English competently, but their speech may still remain hard to understand because they do not use syllabic stress appropriately, especially in long words, such as "individual," "thermometer," or "photography." They probably learned these words with their eyes (the written language), not their ears (the spoken language). This lack of ease with the intonation pattern of American English is frequently what makes them sound "foreign" to us.

Infants in any culture learn the song their people sing—the intonation patterns characteristic of their mother tongue—within the very first year of life, before they are capable of understanding, much less using words. This learning is early and provides a strong foundation for the acquisition of spoken language.

There can be problems. American-born individuals may be producing a stream of syllables that aren't exactly without inflection but with minimal energy, resulting in a rather boring and monotone speech delivery. The rare colleague, student, or parishioner may speak up and tell the individual that they would do well to develop livelier speech, but it is rare that people will risk seeming rude. More often the individual will hear a recording and be horrified at the dull delivery. That flat tone is not at all what they intended. In their own minds they are lively fellows indeed. And they do know how to melodically present a sentence. They just need reminding of the patterns and convincing them that they need to give these patterns more energy.

What is stress anyway? You make a more energized syllable. You're going to think that it is louder, and yes, that is so. But it also is probably a longer syllable and might even be pitched slightly higher than the other syllables. There's just more of this syllable than its neighbors. If you say, "We'll go to Mars someday," notice what you do with that word "Mars." Isn't it louder, longer, and higher? If we were to indicate this primary stress on paper, we would put a mark like this " in front of it: "Mars.

People from other language backgrounds need specific training in the sound patterns of American English. I use *Intonation Patterns of American English* by Sikorski to provide intensive homework in hearing and copying the stress patterns in words.

If you are sometimes described as monotonous or boring in speech delivery, it is a good idea to spend some time developing your awareness and use of intonation patterns. No other single feature can improve your intelligibility as much as this.

Developing Awareness of Primary and Secondary Stress

"This is the 'way / I 'want you to "talk. The " in front of *this* and *talk* directs you to put more emphasis on that syllable, and the ' indicates that *way* and *want* would receive somewhat less stress.

Say the practice sentence, *This is the way I want you to talk,* and use the stress pattern indicated above. We want to hear a slight difference between the primary and secondary levels of emphasis. You might want to ask some external ears if you are successful in following these markings.

Now try the follow sentences:

She be'came a "bank president.

I 'think I'll "go to "school to'morrow.

My 'sister "Mary wants a 'blue "Honda.

I "ordered 'lemon 'cream "pie.

Notice how we indicate meaning just with our choice of stress:

'She is a 'smart "girl. (This is a statement of
fact.)

'She is a "smart 'girl. (But she acts silly.)

"She is a "smart 'girl. (But her sister is not.)

'She is a "smart "girl. (She is really smart.)

'She "is a 'smart "girl. (No matter what you say
to the contrary.)

We do a lot of our subtle communication through just
such patterns of relative emphasis. They provide countless
opportunities for shades of meaning—innuendo, hints, and
suggestion—without outright word choices. Vocabulary can
be easily quoted, but it's somewhat more difficult for most
people to quote an intonation.

Wife looks fixedly at husband preparing to go out to dinner.
"You're wearing *that* shirt?" He knows immediately that he
has made a huge error here. He is taken aback. "What's wrong
with it?" She responds, all innocence (eyes wide open, wrists
exposed), "Oh, I didn't say anything was wrong. I was just asking!" Yeah, right.

It's a good idea to spend some time noticing intonation patterns in the mouths of melodic speakers on recordings, which
enable you to play a phrase repeatedly so you can really listen
for the patterning and get beyond the literal meaning being
conveyed. This is an easier task than trying to catch the subtle
verbal music flying by your ear in real time. Actual speaking
triggers meaning. You need to focus completely on the actual
music of the language being spoken.

People you have met already in this book—Michelle (stereotyped sentence patterning), Joan (singsong), Fernando (fast),
Reid (indecisive), Jimmy (inarticulate), and Marilyn (adolescent patterns)—were all individuals who worked on their
intonation awareness and development as part of their speech
improvement efforts. It was especially helpful in getting them

to be aware of how their bodies were important in expressing meaning. Like many really smart people, "meaning"
was pretty much an intellectual thing that did not get sufficiently realized in their own bodily movement patterns so it
could be expressed to others. You will recall that communication always involves the consideration of the listener.

I will mark emphasis on the first three lines below. You finish the piece.

> Our "deepest fear is "not that we are in'adequate.
> Our "deepest fear is that we are "powerful be"yond
> "measure. It is our "light, not our 'darkness, that
> "most 'frightens us.
>
> We ask ourselves, Who am I to be brilliant, gorgeous,
> talented, and fabulous? Actually, who are you not to
> be? You are a child of God. Your playing small does
> not serve the world. There's nothing enlightened
> about shrinking so that other people won't feel
> insecure around you. We are all meant to shine, as
> children do. We were born to make manifest the
> glory of God that is within us. It's not just in some
> of us; it's in everyone. And as we let our own light
> shine, we unconsciously give other people permission
> to do the same. As we're liberated from our own fear,
> our presence automatically liberates others.

(This passage by Marianne Williamson is frequently misidentified as the 1994 inaugural speech of Nelson Mandela.
But it's still a great speech.)

The music of speaking is an important feature of poetry.
Let's look at the following poem, "Unfortunate Coincidence"
by Dorothy Parker, and feel the rhythm of the language. Here
is how I might read it:

> By the "time you swear you're "his,
> 'shivering and 'sighing
> And he "vows his 'passion is
> "Infinite, un"dying—
> "Lady, make a 'note of this:
> "One of you is 'lying.

What's your favorite poem? Can you get a copy, say it out loud, and figure out the emphasis pattern?

Remember the Gettysburg Address earlier in the book? In addition to the phrasing, figure out the emphasis pattern that makes sense to you.

You may recall Reid, who received the unfortunate performance review about his "deficits in communication skills." His work included giving a brief report at a weekly committee meeting. Fortunately for our work together, he could bring the written report so we could analyze for phrasing and stress patterns, mark the written report accordingly, read it aloud several times for fluency, and end with a spoken version that was very easy on the ear.

Reid went to these meetings with much more confidence that he could present himself with clarity and assurance. Moreover, he learned that he could continue his success by just taking the time to consider intonation patterns before he ever presented. He told me he would "doodle" over his written remarks, making little slashes and emphasis notes. And he wouldn't necessarily have to look at the written material to remind himself; just the act of thinking it through seemed to be of great help to him.

The Overly Emphatic Person

Some people hit their stressed syllables very hard. "I do NOT want to even THINK about the possiBILity of a LAWsuit." We are not talking about the staccato pattern here that involves vowel initiation, but the whole syllable, no matter how it starts. People with little variation in stress may be somewhat hard to understand, but there is no problem understanding the overly emphatic person. The meaning and the attitude come through loud and clear. When these syllables of natural stress are hit exceptionally hard, it reveals something of a Type A personality, an aggressive kind of sound. You feel that they are authoritarian or dictatorial. You won't find the evidence in *what* they say, but in *how* they say it.

If you are this overly emphatic as a speaker, you probably don't know it. You may intend to say, "I really don't want you to do that," as the reasonable fellow you are. But what is heard is, "I really *DON'T* want you to DO that!" Your listener will feel it and respond to the emotional tone.

Overemphasis and the hard edges of staccato talkers can cause interpersonal problems in the workplace, problems that are nigh impossible for the involved individuals to figure out. "I don't know, there's just something about the way she talks that is so off-putting!" says Kristen's boss. "People do not want to work with her." When I interviewed Kristen, this pattern was not really noticeable at first, but as she began telling me about the problems at work, the tension in her voice became apparent and I heard the explosive syllables increasingly.

Since you can't fix it if you don't hear it, I played the recording for Kristen, pointing out examples of the emphasis pattern that was bothering people. She couldn't hear it. She could only hear what she meant to say, not *how* she said it. She took every listening example as an opportunity to justify what she had said. And she remained deeply convinced that the people at work just had it in for her.

It has been said that the meaning of a communication is in the response it gets. When there is a marked difference between what you meant and what was apparently heard, you should entertain the idea that maybe you put a spin on it with your pattern of intonation or emphasis. If you frequently catch yourself in the self-justification ("All I said was ...") explaining that the other person simply overreacted, use it as a cue that you may be in denial of your attitudinal communication.

What happened to Kristen? Since I could not assure Kristen's employer that she was a good candidate for change, she was offered an early retirement.

Having Fun with Your Syllables!

Yes, you can. I am including an exercise that might make you aware of the importance of the subtle timing relationships between syllables and how they completely change the meaning of the statement. Read the following sentences aloud, putting a slight pause in the sentence as marked. Then change the sentences to mean something different by relocating the pauses and stress pattern. In the first example, is this a man who is eating a shark, or a shark that likes to snack on people?

> A man / eating shark. A man eating shark.
>
> The blind man / picked up his hammer / and saw. The blind man picked up his hammer and saw.
>
> The waiter / always serves our food / and drinks in the dining room. The waiter always serves our food and drinks in the dining room.
>
> He sells pink ladies' / gloves. He sells pink ladies' gloves.
>
> The architect / draws driveways / and walks in circles. The architect draws driveways and walks in circles.
>
> The waiter / always serves our coffee / and rolls downstairs. The waiter always serves our coffee and rolls downstairs.
>
> Let's eat / Mother. Let's eat Mother.

I hope you can see now that the way we speak conveys much of our meaning. These are subtle, hard-to-define features of speaking, but aren't they fascinating?

Developing the Resonant Voice

"I could listen to him all day. I just love the sound of his voice!" More than likely the sound she loves is probably a rich, melodic, chest voice. Let's take a look at that "chest" part.

We start with a distinction between "head" and "chest" voice. A few seconds of actual demonstration would quickly make this point, but bear with me through this anemic visual medium. The head voice is a young sound, thin, emanating from the front of the face. It is the natural sound of a ten-year-old. In an adult, this voice can sound thin and childlike. Add in a few more factors and you may even use the words "whining" or even "strident."

Jeremy was recently hired by a large company to be a sales representative. His performance review included comments about "youthfulness" that he interpreted as meaning "immaturity." When I called his boss to get clarification, his boss specifically mentioned a "boyish, high voice."

Jeremy was, indeed, a young man getting started in the business world. He was excited about his first job and looking for ways to excel. Jeremy was a likeable person, bright and fun and an eager beaver, radiating lots of goodwill and energy. His voice and demeanor was indeed youthful, but Jeremy's voice itself was not high. It was placed in the front of his face and just sounded high because of the overtones. He needed to develop the richer resonances of his throat to balance the brighter sounds from the front of his face.

As for chest voice, it is usually lower pitched, of course, but the important aspect is really the deeper resonance you hear from the body of the speaker. And that is the crucial feature. You hear the sound of the body, notably the throat and chest, evident in the voice. Listen to Richard Burton. Listen to Lauren Bacall. Listen to James Earl Jones. These voices are very physical in their resonance patterns, messages from the interior of the body, and this is exactly what makes them compelling. It is a sound of maturity and composure.

If you want to check the sound of your own voice, it really helps to record your conversation with other people. Does *their* recorded voice sound much like it does to you coming through the air? How does your voice sound relative to the other people (of the same sex)? Try to focus just on the sound of your voice, not content, rate, etc.

You can also cup your hands behind your ears while you talk and you will get a better idea of how your voice might sound. An old-fashioned way of amplifying your voice is to use an open shoe box held beside your mouth and ear while you talk. Try it.

One way of checking on your chest resonance is to put your hand on your sternum (that bone in the middle of your upper chest) and glide your voice up and down in your lower tones, like singing little scales up and down. Feel for a sense of vibration under your hand. This exercise can help direct your attention to the feeling of chest vibration. You want this.

Here are some of the things Jeremy did that might help you.

Yawn and feel how the back of your throat pops open in a genuine yawn; you want this more open throat. Deliberately focus your attention on it. Try to maintain the awareness of the sensation so you can learn to replicate it intentionally. Jeremy noticed immediately how different this posture felt compared to his usual pattern of constriction in the back of his throat. He said it felt like he just drank some cold lemonade that he really enjoyed.

Keep your tongue flat in your mouth so the tip touches the back of your lower teeth. (Your impulse will be to pull your tongue back in your throat. Resist!) You want to feel your throat as open and relaxed as possible. Breathe through your mouth and try to feel the air sliding in the open space of your throat.

Produce a singing tone that starts high and glides lower, imagining it going down into your chest. It should sound and feel different from your normal voice if you've maintained the openness of your mouth and throat. You might place your hand in the middle of your upper chest and try to feel the vibrations from these lower resonances.

Do the same up and down scales, but singing "gah" with each note, you'll be positioning your tongue better for voice production. Make your vowel like the word "awe" for the best resonance features. This vowel will open your mouth and lower your jaw if you are doing it right.

Take a peek at yourself in the mirror and see if you are moving your jaw in this exercise or if you tend to keep your mouth fairly closed. Moving and open is good; closed is bad. You could put a finger or two in your mouth (vertically) to see if you are dropping your jaw enough to generate good oral resonance. You should be able to hear a much bigger sound. Note how this feels and how it differs from your usual tone. What may strike you as loud may actually be just a richer sound with more harmonic energy than you are used to hearing. Consult your friend the recorder.

Maintaining the lower pitch, go "Hohoho" like the Jolly Green Giant, letting the tone come from deep in the chest. Repeat. Pay attention to the feeling in the throat as you make this big relaxed sound with no strain. The Jolly Green Giant was a useful concept for Jeremy to locate the resonances in the back of his throat—a place he had never visited before!

Of course, you now must do the practice to make it a familiar place for you to use in your speaking. If you have never even heard of the Jolly Green Giant, you might use Santa Claus as an image. If you have never had an image of Santa Claus, how about Darth Vadar (otherwise known as James Earl Jones)? But without the creepy breathing sounds.

Most speech sounds have a vocalic element (your voice), not just the vowels. If you could do one thing to make your speaking more pleasant and compelling, it would be to have more actual voice present in your speaking—with vowels enriched with more energy and distinctiveness. The concept of tonal support is probably the single most important technique in producing a beautiful voice, and it has everything to do with keeping that vocal tone clearly humming along during your speaking.

We have become heavy users of consonants, the "noise" elements of articulation. These are the speech sounds that depend on constriction, pressure, and air (say *k, s,* or *ch,* for example; the actual speech sounds themselves, not the name of the sounds). Many people seem to speak with a mouth full of these constrictive sounds with their vowels diminished and colorless. More vowel energy (tonal support) gives you clear distinctive information ("pin" or "pen"?); increased vocal resonance (a richer sound); enhanced melody line (pitch variation); and more sense of being relationship oriented.

Let's energize your voice:

Hum. Let your lips touch loosely, teeth not clamped shut. Wrap your hand around the front of your throat and feel the vibration. That's your voice, produced by the vibration of two small muscles behind that bony cartilage in the front of your neck. Your breath stream, coming up from the lungs into the windpipe, causes these little muscles to vibrate. But the humming sound should feel like it is happening throughout the whole of your oral mechanism.

Let's take a line from Old MacDonald now and say "ee-ai-ee-ai-oh" so that the vowels come out in a continuous stream. If your hand is on your throat, you should feel a steady stream of voice unaffected by the movement in your jaw, tongue, and lips, as if you were singing. Notice how much movement is happening in your mouth as you position your tongue to produce different vowels. In general, poor speakers do not move their articulators enough for really clear speech. The more weird this feels to you, the more likely that you are in the "poor speaker" category. Go to the corner immediately. And hum.

Now say "to be my own" as if it were one word, with your hand on your throat. It should feel like the hum or the "ee-ai-ee-ai-oh," a steady vibration. I hope you notice that saying a phrase like this (as if it were one word) is the natural preferred way of linking one word to the next. This is *not* incorrect articulation; it is smooth connected speech. You actually get more consonants heard this way.

Repeat the phrase several times, producing the underlined vowels as distinctly as possible: "t*o* b*e* m*y* *o*wn" (*oo ee ai oh*), but keeping the sound connected.

Try another: "M*y* n*a*me *i*s J*oa*n." Pay attention to vowel identity (*ai ay ih oh*).

Make up a short sentence of your own and say it in the same way: keeping your voice continuous and paying attention to making your vowels distinctly.

If you think "singing," you will probably find this exercise easier to do. Because, really, it is the same mechanism and concept of flow that both singing and beautiful speaking have in common. There is more vocal tone when you produce words so your syllables are fatter (so to speak) and we hear the distinctive vowel color.

Pretend you're speaking Italian. This language has a lovely balance of consonants and vowels that lends itself to beautiful speech. Why do you think they invented opera?

If you put your hand on your throat and sing (something like "Oh, what a beautiful morning," for example), you should feel a steady stream of vibration called "tonal support." It's what I want you to develop for your speaking voice. Now, talk in your normal fashion for a while with your hand on your throat and determine how the vibration pattern differs from what you felt during the singing. Focus your attention on what you are doing and be willing to put some time into it. Your vocal use during speech should not be that much different from singing. This continuing stream of tonality creates a physical presence in your speech that is melodic, rich, and resonant.

Developing Tonal Support

Gliding from one syllable/word to the next may strike you as sloppy speech but it is not. Done correctly, all sounds will be heard even though they are part of a larger phrasal unit. (I know I've already said this; you need to hear it twice.)

Say the phrases below as if they were one word, one continuous flow. Keep sound in front of your mouth. And don't forget all that good work you just did with vowel identity.

Many men.

I love you.

Lovely one.

How are you? (Some people use glottal attack, with strong emphasis on "are"—you don't need to do that.)

Deal me in. (Don't use glottal attack on "in.")

Do you feel okay?

Matter of fact.

Wind in the willows. (Don't use glottal attack on "in." Think of it as "win-din.")

Read and practice the following sentences using the same instructions as before. Then, get your eyes off the page and say the sentences from memory. Even close your eyes to help you concentrate on the sound and feel of this practice.

My name is unusual.

One alone to be my own.

We can whenever we want to.

My place will do for now.

It's a great idea to record yourself doing this and to compare your recorded voice to your usual usage. You want to hear a smooth, well-articulated sound, rather than choppy staccato.

Read these additional sentences, and then say them out loud concentrating on tonal support, vowel clarity, and different pitch intonations.

Maybe my niece will want some.

Why would we follow him?

Would you want to do it?

None of us would want to.

Wait where we will find you.

Where is my mother?

We know you're in there.

What time is it?

Don't ask about it.

John always eats apples.

Ask if it's all right.

We haven't heard anything.

Don't expect him.

They reject about half the first semester.

When you feel confident that you have mastered these sentences, get your eyes up and your butt off the chair! Do the sentence work as you move around the room, getting your vocal work coordinated with your whole body movement. Your speaking is a physical act that must be integrated with your whole body as it moves in space and time in the real world. Do not repeat mindlessly, but keep your attention deliberately focused so you can learn something from the exercise. When you get distracted, stop.

Of course, it's time to start working with material that pertains to your particular needs. As usual, use short phrases, go slow, get your eyes up, etc.

As Jeremy used these techniques, on his feet, with his work-related material, we started calling it his "Big Dog" voice (as opposed to the "Puppy" voice). This became an extremely useful way to characterize the two forms of voice production and actually made it easier for him to differentiate between them. So we would practice some material in Puppy and then switch to Big Dog. Then switch back. He was developing a sense of control of his voice.

This led to an important insight for Jeremy when he tried to carry over the more resonant voice to his workplace. He could use his Big Dog voice just fine with new sales contacts, but when he needed to communicate with his supervisor, he found himself reverting to Puppy. This revealed to him the huge psychological component of the sound of our voice in our relationships. What he could do physically, he couldn't do emotionally. He had to really own that Big Dog voice, a part of his growing up.

We added three features to our carryover work:

1. He would do daily excursions to practice with neutral ears to build his confidence.

2. He would aim at having just one very short exchange with his supervisor every day in his Big Dog voice, perhaps just a friendly "How are you?" in the morning. Then he would build on that.

3. And he would try to leave the Puppy at home more often.

Getting It Pitch Perfect

The sound of your voice reflects your physical and psychological characteristics. You will recall from "High Talkers" that people can hear the sound of your voice and usually get a fairly accurate idea of your sex and age from the physical dimensions of both your vocal cords and the length and width of your speaking mechanism.

But there are also features of learning and habit that influence how you use your speaking mechanism. Pitch is one of those features that is subject to both psychological needs and conscious manipulation. You can understand why we would try to influence our pitch level; pitch carries some heavy psychological freight!

Since many of us are not skilled at judging the adequacy or normalcy of our own vocal pitch usage, I urge you to get a knowledgeable assessment from some trusted external ears.

Remember that "high" and "low" are relative terms when we are speaking about the voice. Your voice may be high relative to one voice but low compared to another. Your judgment must be made in the context of other voices in your sex and age group.

The most common pitch-related problem I hear in my work is that of a restricted, gravelly voice, pitched at the very bottom of the person's range, a very strained and unhealthy voice that does not carry or project your words. sounds scratchy and unpleasant. irritates the vocal folds. and reduces vocal dynamics.

This issue is discussed at length in "Raspy Talkers."

Rather than trying to lower your voice, how about finding the most comfortable and appropriate pitch for your physical structure, the one right for you?

Find some trusted external ears who have some musical abilities. Have them ask you questions to which the answer is "yes" but you say "um hum" instead:

Did you come by car? "Um hum."

Are you wearing blue today? "Um hum."

The friend will listen carefully to this "um hum" sound to extract a pitch from it. Try not to do a big pitch change between the two syllables. And slow it down a bit so you can really hear the pitch level of the sound.

Now try to prolong the tone you are using for your "um hum" by singing or humming it. Can you find it on a keyboard? Try finding a piano keyboard on your computer if you don't have the real thing. Perhaps you or your friend have the ear to determine the pitch of your tone; give it a try. Once you find a match on the keyboard, try to sing down a few tones lower. If the pitch you were *um humming* on turns out to be the lowest tone you can produce, move your pitch up at least two whole notes on the keyboard. You want to have a margin of voice capacity below your modal or average pitch to allow for intonation patterning. About two or three notes above the bottom (comfortable) note is a pitch level that is probably unstrained and appropriate to use as your average pitch level.

These exercises are equally helpful if you have been using a higher pitch level than is optimal. Continue through the following sentence work using this pitch level you have discovered in the previous exercise. Then record this sentence work and compare the recording to your original voice sample. This comparison will tell you what you need to know.

Once you get to the appropriate tone, add some syllables, keeping the pitch level the same throughout. Let's say you are humming; you might go, "mmmmm-one-one-one-one" or "hmmmm-many-many-many," keeping a continuous tone. (You might hum at one pitch but start chanting words on a different pitch, so watch for this.)

Put your hand around your throat (gently) so you can feel the steady vibration of your voice during these exercises. There should be no catches or stoppages when you are vocalizing. Just let the vocal folds vibrate in a comfortable but sustained tone.

After you are successful with this exercise (be patient!) do the same routine using some short sentences on this comfortable vocal pitch. Here are some examples:

> *The early bird deserves to get the worm.*
>
> *Freedom is what you do with what's been done to you.*
>
> *No one can make you feel inferior without your consent.*
>
> *Today is the tomorrow I was waiting for.*

Get your tone established, and go into your sentence maintaining that same pitch you've been working with: *Hmmmmm-the-early-bird-deserves-to-get-the-worm.*

Pay attention to that one ideal pitch; notice and ignore the impulse to shift back into your habitual pitch. Maintain that one tone across the whole sentence.

When you are confident that you can keep the pitch level you have discovered, start introducing normal pitch variation toward the end of the sentence. So you start by chanting the words (the underlined words are your base, ideal pitch):

```
                          get (Go up in pitch.)
                        /
Hmmm the-early-bird-deserves-to
                        \
                          the worm. (Go down below
                                     your chanted tone.)
```

Go through all the short sentences using the same procedure, allowing pitch variation on the last three to five words. The idea here is to hold your general pitch level in the area around the note we are working with. You will notice if it feels sort of normal to you or not. You can make up your own simple sentences for practice.

Note: As soon as you start to feel fatigued or distracted, stop and take a break. Come back later in the day, and do another ten minutes or so. Practice like this is fatiguing on a deep level (it may not seem that hard to do, but it actually takes a good deal of energy and concentration), so get away. Just be sure to come back to it later with renewed attention and energy. After this material seems easy for you, go on to the next step.

Now, allow more of the sentence to vary in intonation. Keep your attention on that first tone to make it stay where you want it to be. There is no "one way" that a sentence *should* be spoken, of course. But it might sound something like this:

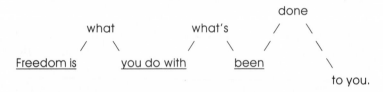

When you have tried this format of more variation with all your sentences, record yourself and then take a break. Give yourself some time off before listening to your recording.

Do not read your sentences while you listen. I'll say it again: your visual system will interfere with your auditory learning. The printed page has no music; only your body does. Use the visual prompts I have included only as long as you need visual guidance. Then disconnect from the page as soon as possible.

Just listen to your original recording and the one you just made. Have a friend listen, too, and discuss what differences you observe and how you like it. Ask yourself: Do you sound comfortable? Age and sex appropriate? Melodic?

That Old Gang of Mine

Meryl was a recent high school graduate. During her last summer break, her parents realized that she had a marked "high school" sound in her speaking that did not connote maturity at all. She was going to her mother's alma mater, and she had visions of social disaster for her daughter. ("*I* never sounded like that! I don't know where she gets it!")

Well, *we* know where she got "it." Adolescence is a period in our lives when we are so susceptible to peer pressure and have the need to look and dress and act and sound like the peer group. Meryl's pitch level was all over the map with an excited, childlike sound. And that's how all her buddies talked, too. Without any lecture or personal critique, I led Meryl through the previous exercises. She was absolutely rapt when we played her final tape. Like most people, she found reason to critique it: "Isn't it too slow? I sound funny, don't I?" Then I played her original tape and her eyes got wider. "Oh. My. God. I can't believe I sounded like that!"

When we relistened to the new tape, she was much more interested in how mature she sounded, more like a woman than a little kid. At this point, she refused to listen to her first tape again. That was not going to be the way she talked anymore. We resumed our work and Meryl made fine progress rapidly. She soon was using her new voice in her home and summer job. When she got back with her high school friends, however, that was another matter!

Now that you see where you're going, apply this practice to increasingly longer sentences. Here's a passage about persistence that I like to work with:

Nothing in the world can take the place of persistence.

Talent will not; nothing is more common than unsuccessful men with talent.

Genius will not; unrewarded genius is almost a proverb.

Education will not; the world is full of educated derelicts.

Persistence and determination alone are omnipotent.

—*Calvin Coolidge*

I would like to imagine that you will first mark the statement for phrasing and emphasis. Then apply the pitch-finding exercise for your oral reading.

Find your own materials from your interests or your work with which to practice. Then start using the phone to extend your practice to talking with other people. Once you feel ready, start using your new pitch with all outgoing calls. Take a few minutes to practice and find your ideal pitch, and then dial. Strangers (neutral ears) are the easiest place to start, so make it a habit to place a call to some store or agency just to practice controlling your pitch. You might use all that time you spend with customer service to do some serious practice.

Carrying a Tune in Your Bucket

The ability to hear and replicate pitch differences is unquestionably important in dealing with vocal dynamics. One of the first things I need to do is determine if my monotone speaker can hear the difference between pitch levels. Many people claim to be tone deaf. Remember Ivan from the Soviet Union?

Are you also one of those people who really would like to sing? From my experience, if you want to sing, you probably can. It will cost you some effort and some teaching, but you can do it. Here's how to start:

First, if you can, get a teacher who will help you hear pitches and produce a proper tone. A voice teacher gives you *appropriate goals* and *knowledgeable support*. Left to yourself, it is likely that you'll quit with the first ungainly squawk out of your throat. A voice professional is far more forgiving than you will be, understanding that it takes lots of squawks and patience to develop a new instrument (your voice).

Second, find a way to play a musical tone and just try to match it with your voice. Take the time to listen carefully to the tone: try to hear it inside your head, and maybe even hum it as you listen. Your complete attention is necessary here. You can start with a telephone dial tone if you have nothing better. You will get better at this with practice. Having an external ear (source of accurate feedback) can help you know if you were successful. If you are at a loss as to how to make your pitch "high" or "low," try swooping your voice up and down in a roller-coaster fashion as best you can, just to get the feel of tightening your vocal cords or relaxing them. This muscle tension information is the key to modifying your pitch knowledge and control.

I would have you raise and lower your arm as you try to make your voice go up and down. Or you could put your hand at the middle of your waist and slide it up to the top of your head as you try to elevate the pitch.

So lock yourself in the bathroom and give it your all.

I sometimes record a tone or an interval on my clients' voice mail or computer so they can access it for their practice at any time. Or I make a practice recording with a piano so they have various tones and intervals (going from one tone to another) to listen to and try to match. They tell me, "Dr. Fleming, I won't be able to do this!" I tell them, "I know, I know. Try it anyway." Their homework is to play their recording several times a day, just focusing on the pitch level of the sounds and trying to match them with their voice. When they bring their recording back and we play it, they assure me that they won't be able to match the tones. But they usually do. (I record that, too.) We listen to this new recording, hearing the matched (or not) tones, asking the clients to decide if they were accurate or not. It takes a while for them to learn to identify a matched tone. Again, by yourself, you'd probably give up. Please remember that Coolidge quote about persistence.

Finally, in the meantime, turn on the radio and sing along uncritically. Do this often, giving yourself the chance to develop auditory-vocal coordinations. And just for the joy of it.

Even If You Can't ...

I heard some great singing at my son's wedding from someone who could not sing—my son. As a surprise for his bride
(and all of us), Jeffrey got up on the stage and "sang" to her "It
Had to be You," which was their song. Everything that makes
a song tuneful, he did not have. What he did have he gave with
all his heart. And it was more than just fine.

CHAPTER 4

Becoming
Well-Spoken

Being well-spoken sounds pretty good, doesn't it? It puts us in a certain class of people who appear to be polished and verbally competent, fluent, gracious, and proper. We all want to be well-spoken, because we know that (1) we judge people by the way they speak, and (2) we want to make a good impression.

To be well-spoken is to be articulate, fluent, and courteous.

Articulate means speaking in a way that is well-formed, clear, and sounds like we mean what we say. It also implies an extensive vocabulary that's appropriate to the situation. The words people use carry information about their intelligence, socioeconomic background, and educational level. The specificity of our vocabulary reveals the distinctions our mind is capable of making. This is why a vocabulary test is a part of almost every intelligence test and why we care about it so much.

Fluent means having words come to us easily and flow effortlessly. There are few extraneous words, sounds, or comments (e.g., ahhh, okay, ya know) that get in the way of straightforward communication. We sense that thought has preceded speaking. Sentences are also well-shaped to easily convey meaning and a consideration of the person being spoken to and a respect for the time of all concerned.

Courteous. There's also a world of courtesy beyond "please" and "thank you" in human discourse that makes a person seem polished. The person with gracious manners is displaying respect and sensitivity to others. Are you just expressing yourself without consideration of the impact on others? Is it possible that you are abrupt? Do you monopolize the conversation? You would probably prefer to be characterized as kind and considerate in your communication style. This is—and can be—learned by starting to notice the social conduct that marks the gracious person.

Fred stated explicitly that he wanted to be well-spoken. He was a man in his late thirties, extremely successful in the investment field, and he dressed beautifully—hair slicked back, hands manicured, and shoes shined. But Fred was ashamed of his speech patterns that had reflected his ethnic and impoverished childhood in New York. To my ear, he had done an excellent job of mastering Standard American English. There was still some work to be done.

Fred had done something else in his determination to change his image, and thus his future. He changed his past. He had gone to an undistinguished public school (we'll call it Public School 12). When the topic of personal histories came up with his current (wealthy and sophisticated) associates, his fellows would cite their experiences at Exeter, Andover, and other prep schools of the wealthy. Fred was embarrassed to mention his roots in PS 12. So he gifted his old school with a sizable donation to build a state-of-the-art science wing, library, and gym. It was a major event in the community. Now when he says he went to PS 12, people say, "I've heard about that place! That's really something!" And Fred was no longer embarrassed by his public school background. With his increased confidence, he was ready to tackle his next challenge: to be well-spoken.

Although you may not have the resources of Fred, you may be equally rich in motivation and energy to becoming well-spoken. There can be no greater investment in your social impact and your personal confidence than fluent, courteous, articulate speaking.

Using the Simple Declarative Sentence

"I want to be alone." "The buck stops here." "I will return."

Welcome to the simple sentence. These short sentences (very Hemingway!) are heard as powerful statements because they're not adulterated by modifiers, clauses, and conjunctions. They are simple statements of fact. They cut to the chase. When you want to be heard as a clear, competent, and forceful person, you want to use more of these short statements of fact.

Compare the following two forms of the same message:

> If you don't mind, it would really work a lot better for all of us if you could manage to be here around eight o'clock because a lot of our customers are on the East Coast and they think nothing of picking up the phone and dealing with their financial issues before our stores are even open. If these people don't get an immediate response they're likely to go elsewhere for their needs and that's going to really hurt our bottom line, and I have no intention of letting that happen on my watch.

> I need you to be here at eight o'clock. Customers will be calling then. It's important to provide prompt service.

Notice how many of the words in the first example actually get in the way of making the point in a clear and forceful manner. Here are some additional ways to use simple, declarative sentences (SDS) to produce more effective communication:

Listen to how people form their sentences and how they marshal their words to express meaning. Concise or verbose? Clear or confusing?

Notice that shorter units of speech are easier for people to *get*, especially in conditions of noise or hurry. You'll be very glad to have these simple sentences to use when you must be definite and forceful with no time to spare. Subject, predicate, period.

Think about every cop show you've seen and the voice of authority when the "bad boys" are caught: *Put your hands in the air. Drop the gun. Turn off the motor.* Think about public safety instructions: *There is a small fire. Do not panic. Doors are at each side of the room. Walk, do not run. Help people who are having trouble. Do not panic. The fire department has arrived.*

Do You Need to Increase Your Power Quotient?

The SDS is associated with confidence, clarity, and authority. While you wouldn't want to *always* use this sentence form, you should examine your own sentence usages to find out if you use it *at all*.

Listen to your recorded conversations and see if you can identify instances of your using the SDS. Can you find places where you wish you had used the stronger sentence form? If so, intentionally repeat the thought in the more verbose way to increase your awareness of it and then reformulate the thought in the SDS.

Look around the room and make up an SDS about what you see. These do not need to be clever. Here are some examples: *The pen is on the table. The window is open. The rug is brown. My telephone is broken. He left his coat. The flowers are dead.*

Practice these short sentences every day in different locales so that it becomes easy for you. Be sure to say them out loud and not just in your head. You need to get that intonation of authority included.

Construct a message using only short sentences (similar to the examples above). Read it out loud using your normal conversational intonation. How does it feel to you? What's missing? Connective language (*... and so ...*)? Fillers (*ya know what I mean*)?

Notice especially if you feel that such abrupt statements are rude or assume too much power. Perhaps you use a lot of softening language to be "nice" and inoffensive.

If you are in a position to write out a speech or some remarks, deliberately look for opportunities to strengthen your statements with the punch and directness of the short sentence interspersed in the longer remarks. Use of the same old sentence format can be monotonous. Changing sentence format will also liven up your remarks. Here is an example:

> Many of us were hoping that Ellie would be able to pull herself away from her desk to be with us. *She cannot.* The deadlines we were concerned about have come home to roost. *She'll stay at her desk. She'll finish the job. We'll see her tomorrow.* I know we're all disappointed and well try to avoid this poor timing in the future. *Thanks for your understanding.*

Social Applications

Consider this situation: You are at a business convention and you are sort of "caught" by a lonely person—let's call her Lee Anne—who will not stop talking. You've tried to break away several times but she doesn't seem to get the message. It just may be that she is simply socially inept or it may be because you have couched your good-bye effort in such disguised language that it is not being received clearly. Now you've just spotted another person who happens to be the exact person you have been hoping to see, a customer that hasn't seen your new product. You turn to chatty Lee Anne and offer your hand for a handshake as you say, "Lee Anne! Good to have met you. I must go. Good night." (Your intonation goes down at the end, and then you walk away.)

If you're wondering, *Isn't that rude?* I'd say, no, it's crisp and definite. This is a business meeting, right? So your job is to go do business. Because Lee Anne has not paid any attention to your previous departure efforts (see "Smooth Small Talk"), the short and direct approach is appropriate.

I hope you noticed that instruction to have your intonation go down at the end of the sentence. If your pitch goes up at the end, as in a question form, you most certainly will not sound as if you really meant it. This "up-ending" is considered by many people to be especially annoying, and you'll want to examine your own recording to see if you use this format very often. Although no one has consulted me to deal with this particular feature in their own speech, you can be sure that it is mentioned by employers when they refer an offending employee.

Words Fail Me!

You know that we make judgments about people's background, intelligence, and education just from the kind of words that come out of their mouths. If you think your own vocabulary has become sloppy—that you used to use many more words but have now fallen into banalities or slang—you share this self-perception with many others. We can turn this around with some insight and effort.

Let's focus our attention on the irritating speech habit of using a noticeable amount of superlatives (coolest) and intensifiers (very). Do you know someone who usually talks like this? "We *just loved* our trip to Europe! It was *really fantastic*, with all the sights and *stuff*. It's *just so* beautiful, you know! *Terrific* food and *everything*." We call this empty language. Can you see why?

Getting control of this habit alone will do a lot to improve your perceived communication skill level.

Empty Language Problem #1

Similar to empty calories, empty language provides no substance but lots of emotional energy. Looking at the first example in the last paragraph, we know without a doubt that this person had a good time. That may be all that really matters to the speaker or even to the listener. But we might also feel that the response is vacuous and self-centered. I think many of us would want to learn at least some specific details of the trip: where exactly did you go, what did you see and do?

Contrast this example with a statement like: "The Serengeti was hot, dry, and enormous. We saw tens of thousands of gnu and zebra in migration. We slept in tents, so it was easy to hear the lions roar at night. I'd go back in a heartbeat!"

Compare the examples and see what there was about the vocabulary that makes these sentences so different. The first example was full of empty intensifiers: "just," "really," and "so." It also had several superlatives: "fantastic" and "terrific." The second example allowed you to share in the experience because you received some specific substantive language.

Pay attention to how other people use words. Do they share meaning or just emotion? Are they thoughtful or thoughtless? Greater awareness of others' language usage will pay off in making you more aware of your own language usage. All change starts with awareness, and you cannot fix what you cannot hear. (You've heard *that* before!)

Intensifiers and superlatives do have a place in our communication. We're talking quantity and appropriateness here. The less you use them, the more meaningful they are. If something relatively common can get you to use "terrific," it indicates that your range of experience is quite limited.

How are you going to find out if *you* use many empty intensifiers or superlatives? Somebody's ears have to focus specifically on the behavior. This will be accomplished by listening to yourself (in recording) or by external ears, professional or not. This will be somewhat difficult for you to catch because you probably do not *always* speak in this fashion and it very well may not have occurred on your recording.

Were you to sit in my office, I might repeat every empty intensifier you use as you speak to help increase your awareness. Do you have a friend who can help you get this awareness?

The first step in changing vocabulary habits is to select a specific word that you want to deal with. Let's say you overdo the word "fantastic." Make up about ten sentences that use "fantastic" the way you usually use it. This is very important. "That was a fantastic movie!" "She had a fantastic time!" Deliberately punch it up to increase your awareness of it.

The second step is to pay attention to when the word naturally slips out of your mouth during talking. What exactly was the sentence you were using? How did it feel to use it? Practice saying the same thing using a different word: "That was a fantastic movie!" or "That was a powerful movie." "That was an interesting movie." "That was an original movie." "That was a thoughtful movie."

In the third step, you should be so sensitized to the word at this point that you become aware of your likelihood of using it just before it happens. It is approaching the tip of your tongue, so to speak, but you catch it, change it, and go on.

Empty Language Problem #2

When you say "uhhh" (where words really fail you), you are treating people to an "empty sound." This is the sound of a laboring train of thought, the sign of buying time while seeking a word. This is totally normal, of course, and we all do it in our everyday talking, especially when we are going after fresh thoughts and new ideas. We don't even notice most of these empty sounds because our attention is in search mode rather than self-monitoring mode.

Ah, but there is one time when all of us really do notice the *uhhh*: when you are giving a speech in front of people. Have you ever found yourself counting the *uhhhs* in someone's presentation? When they are many, and especially if they are loud, they call attention to themselves and become distracting and irritating.

Do your thinking and word selection *before* you speak in public. This is the difference between a smooth presentation, which demonstrates respect for an audience, and just winging it, which doesn't. Prepare your remarks and review them several times; the words will follow one another more fluently because they have done so before.

The most important place to practice for fluency is when transitioning from one thought or paragraph to the next. This is a place where *uhhh* lurks. Think through the language you will use going from one thought to another. You'll be so glad you did this.

You must find a way to develop awareness of when you tend to insert these fillers, or empty sounds. Practice your speech with a friend who will immediately drop a marble in a tin can every time he hears the filler. Yes, this will drive you nuts, and yes, it will quickly make you aware when you do it again. It won't take long to break this habit if your friend is good at spotting all the little *uhhhs* leaking out of your speech and giving you rapid feedback.

Now you can turn around and drop marbles on your friend who probably could also use the help. Paying close attention to the filler in someone else's speech also helps you in gaining awareness of your own.

Improving Your Vocabulary with Your Ears

The most efficient way to build your vocabulary will likely sound outrageous: Socialize with people who have a better education and a more developed language than the folks you usually see. This may be a bit of a stretch for you, but you can't beat the stimulation to your vocabulary (and your brain and your life) any other way. I understand how much more comfortable you will be with your old pals, and heaven knows there's a place for social comfort. But there is also a place for vocabulary stimulation. They may not be the same place.

Your current language usage pretty much reflects your intelligence, your socioeconomic milieu as a child, your educational and occupation, and the stimulation and needs of your quotidian life. (Have you noticed that you've picked up some of the current expressions used by your children?)

When you spend time with different people of achievement and education, you will be exposed to words you don't know; and you can learn these words just as a child does by being exposed to them, actively noticing and repeating them, remembering the context of usage, and trying to use them.

As an adult, you can ask speakers about the words they use that you don't know. You probably think that people will look down on you for this, but not so. People will admire your desire to learn and your willingness to ask (and probably will be flattered to share their wisdom).

Vocabulary Building with Your Eyes

I picked up a small book about public speaking that was on sale at my local library (fifty-four cents). As I skimmed the pages, I noticed small inked dots on some of the words (fey, cull, covet), thirty-four marked words in all. Page 24 received the last of the dots (recoil, larded). The book went on to 109 pages with some pretty good words (rigor mortis, preemptory, verdant), but the previous reader was no longer marking words or had stopped reading altogether. Now, why would anyone make dots over certain words? And with a ballpoint pen?

I choose to believe that the person was noting words that he or she did not know. It revealed a hungry mind seeking out new meaning. However, there was no evidence of the second step: finding out how to pronounce and use the word. The flyleaves in the book would have been a good place to make such notes.

Finding a new word in your reading material is the ideal time to learn that word because it is in the context that will most likely reveal elements of its meaning. Use this opportunity to do the following:

Note and mark the word. Copy the word in your own handwriting. For example, copy the word g-e-r-m-a-n-e.

After consulting a dictionary to determine pronunciation, *write your own version of the spoken form*—perhaps "jer MAIN"—*and what it means* (truly relevant). No, I don't think a keyboard stroke has the same learning potential as a handwritten word. Write a sentence that actually uses the words: "His comments were not germane to the topic." You could also write down the page where you found it used in the book—for example, "Page 20: You needn't reject a germane subject because you have only a few things worth saying about it."

So far you're all by yourself with a book and a pencil. You've done what you can to intellectually appreciate the word. But words have to be actually manufactured by your body to become part of you.

Read your sentences aloud, and then repeat your sentence without looking at the written form. Concentrate on tasting the word in its verbal context.

Now you will want to actually *use it a couple of times to truly own it*. Do you have a friend you could call and try it out? Why not have a designated vocabulary buddy who understands what you're trying to do and will cooperate in some trial usage? With this kind of say-it-out-loud practice, what comes in through the eyes can come out in your speech. And isn't that the idea?

Other Vocabulary Sources

Use your computer to *visit online vocabulary-building sites.* I recommend FreeRice.com. This vocabulary-building site is a rice distribution site. For every correct word you get, twenty grains of rice are given to the hungry through the UN World Food Program. The site also shows you how to pronounce the word. So don't footle! Try it out. It's fun!

Sign up for a daily new word at Merriam-Webster.com. The word comes with pertinent and interesting information about the usage and history of the word. You can also access their dictionary, of course.

Go to Amazon.com, and then search "vocabulary" in the Audiobook department. You will find recorded vocabulary-building material for purchase, from *Comic Vocab: Laugh Your Way to a Better Vocabulary* to the *Princeton Review Word Smart* series of books. Your local library and bookstores will have some recorded material that is designed for language learners from other countries (English as a Second Language) but little for the native-born student, unless you are preparing for your SAT.

Look the word up in a printed dictionary or in an online source, such as Wikipedia. Write the meaning in your own words so you can remember it and won't have to look it up again. Better yet, invest in a workbook that is designed to help you learn the usage of the words. Try *1100 Words You Need to Know* by Bromberg and Gordon. If you don't want to know that many more words, try *504 Absolutely Essential Words* by Bromberg, Lieber, and Traeger.

Speaking Your Mind Effectively

Do you know the difference between someone who is just talking and someone who is talking to you? Of course you do. It's a feeling of interpersonal connection.

Let's say you have asked some accomplished individual about a topic he has just mentioned. He—the rocket scientist, brain surgeon, computer programmer—launches into an erratic stream of language laced with jargon, interrupted sentences, fragmented thoughts, and punctuated with high speed and averted eyes. This man is trying to put his thoughts into language, and all his attention is focused on just that. You feel as if you are sitting in the backseat of a car—blindfolded—as he drives on a mountain road, careening from side to side with mysterious turns and twists. The speaker relieves himself of whatever popped into his head, but you are left mystified, irritated, or feeling stupid. He has expressed himself. (On my scratch pad I would draw a stick figure with a popcorn popper as a head, little thought kernels flying every which way.)

Come to think of it, you don't have to be a rocket scientist to talk this way. You could just be a person dealing with new concepts and information and have not yet figured out which way is up.

Self-Expression vs. Communication

What is *self-expression*? It means you say what you want to say in the manner that comes to you naturally. It will be your take on the matter, in the words you normally use, perhaps with the narrative flow of your experience. It's a solo performance in front of people with 100 percent of *your* attention on finding and speaking *your* thoughts, as opposed to *communication* where the listener is foremost in your mind as you speak.

Communication will feel like direct involvement with your listeners. You speak their language, you speak to their concerns, and you get to the point insofar as it concerns *them*. You read their response even as you speak (thus the importance of eye contact in conversation and public speaking). If this kind of consideration can become a habit with you, your communication skills—public and private—will advance markedly.

Most of us are pretty good at this in a one-on-one situation. It's usually the group situations that throw us.

If you think you may be high on self-expression and a bit low on communication, here is your own seven-step program to apply in both business and social settings. It starts with a genuine desire to communicate (which means "to make common") with people.

1. Take time to figure out the interest/knowledge level of your listener. If someone asked you for directions to some place, you would need to know where they are *now*, wouldn't you? You need to know their general familiarity with the area to efficiently lead them from point A to point B. You may have to play mind reader here or ask a few initial exploratory questions. Be alert to all the information you can glean from the interaction to pick the most appropriate response to create a genuine connection with this particular person.

2. Choose appropriate vocabulary. When you think about all the ways that people are different from each other, it's a wonder we can communicate at all! But more wonderful yet is our fabulously developed language that enables us to choose our words to fit the circumstance. A summary for your neighbor is going to sound different from a report to your boss; the data dump for your

colleague must differ from the social chat with the new hire. The use of highly technical language to a nontechnical person not only puzzles him but can make him feel stupid, thus creating huge and unnecessary distances between people (like you and your mother).

3.   References to occupation are a common feature of most introductions. Many occupations in science and technology have become so specialized that they defy easy description to the layperson. Your title or general job description may well serve as a barrier rather than a bridge to other people outside your industry ("I'm a computer architect"). You need to construct that bridge by searching for images and experiences that your listener has had that might help you describe your work. Even if your work is nontechnical ("I'm a lab assistant"), some fleshing out with actual descriptive language helps your listener know you better ("I make sure that the blood and urine samples are properly labeled, entered into the log, and delivered to the lab for analysis, among other things"). Let me give you an example from my work as a personal communication coach. If asked about my work, I would gauge my answer for the person asking, like this:

> To a stay-at-home individual: "You know how a lot of people can't stand their voice on a recording?" (She nods.) "Well I'm the person that helps them improve the sound of their voice."

> To a seven-year-old boy: "Are there boys and girls in your class that don't talk as well as other kids?" (He nods.) "Well, I'm the kind of teacher that helps them talk really well."

To a corporate executive: "I coach corporate executives how to be concise and powerful in their communications."

Notice that I'm telling them what I *do*, not who I am.

4. If you know you're going to be presenting information, *think first so it can be organized in a manner conducive to easy comprehension* (see the chapter "Getting Your Point Across"), and avoid subjecting other people to your awkward on-the-spot formulations. People do not like to sit through your hemming and hawing, sentence revisions, and repetitions. Don't take them into the kitchen when they just want the cake.

5. Make it safe for people to ask for clarification. Many people nod and smile and just hope to get to the end of the conversation without revealing that they are totally in the dark. There is the possibility of a serious misunderstanding with real consequences when the listener is too embarrassed to admit that he is snowed. Ethnic and cultural differences (including disinclination to admitting a lack of understanding) can also add additional danger to the assumption of a shared vocabulary.

6. Get to the point immediately when speaking with decision makers. If they want data or detail, they'll ask for it. They'll have only so much attention for you so you must think of economy of presentation. If you can respect their time, they're likely to respect your mind.

7. Select your small talk thoughtfully in social conversation. Chatting is the time for short

pleasantries with speaking opportunities passing back and forth, much like the volley in a tennis game. Don't embark on detailed information, any story over 5 minutes in length, or anything intricate. These require a follow-up meeting to allow more focused attention. Social situations are for people interaction, not long monologues.

If you are willing to invest 50 percent of your attention in your listener/audience, you'll get a 100 percent reception from them.

Offering a Gracious Response

Leo suffered so much in social interactions that he had to admit to himself that he must be doing something wrong. He stood miserable and tongue-tied, locked in silence, while other people actually talked to each other. While he knew he could not break the ice, he didn't know that he was pushing the glacier in front of him. Other people felt no warmth and welcome from him, so of course, they avoided him.

Leo had to deal with the very first assumptions of social interaction: kindness, courtesy, consideration, and graciousness. Now you might think that this would be a strange area for instruction, but there are people so wrapped up in their own self-consciousness and discomfort that just thinking about being nice to other people doesn't come to mind.

Leo needed to learn exactly what was meant by "politeness" and how it was communicated. Politeness is trickier than you might think. It starts with an attitude at once warm and respectful.

People need to feel *respect* for their physical and psychological space. Their barriers must be discerned and honored. This means that you do not touch them other than to offer your hand for a grasp and that you address them with their titles (if appropriate) and last name. In formal or business settings, you make no assumptions of intimacy or familiarity until they give you expressed permission to do so ("Can I call you Joe?").

People need to feel *warmth*, welcome, and a sense that you are pleased to see them. For this, we give them eye contact and a smile. We extend a clean hand with a firm and complete grasp of theirs. We say something like, "How do you do?" "I'm pleased to meet you," etc. Our voice needs to sound sincere.

There is an important distinction between warmth and respect. This line varies between cultures and people. Do not assume that all people are to be approached in the same way. Look for the signals that other people are sending that tell you about their comfort level. You might take a look at the sad story of Ms. Refined, Ms. Lively, and their nonverbal differences in the section on "Smooth Small Talk."

The gracious person offers warmth without violating the other's need for respect. Leo was so paralyzed by his own emotional isolation that the very concept of offering kindness, courtesy, and consideration to the other person astonished him. He was incredulous: *he* should be trying to make other people feel welcome and comfortable? What a novel idea!

What helped Leo was to teach him specific behaviors he could practice to start melting his own ice. Here is the scenario that we started with to help Leo become more forthcoming and positive when meeting new people.

Suppose you are a single person attending the wedding of a friend. You do not know anybody else. At the reception, a person approaches you and says, "Are you a friend of the groom?" (And you are.) More than likely this is just a conversational opener and a display of friendly intent. Lucky you, someone has graciously taken the initiative to get the ball rolling to get to know you better.

Suppose you answer "Yes." Now what? Depending on the context and tone of voice, this simple "yes" could actually be heard as a rude dismissive response. Consider it from their point of view: You gave the most minimal of answers. as if the person simply wanted the information (in what is obviously a social context), and you probably forced this nice person to come up with another question if, in fact, she was trying to develop a conversational relationship with you.

What if you answered, "Yes, I am." Can you feel that this is somehow a friendlier answer? It's like taking the offered handshake with a warm responsive grip. "Yes, I am" (a friend of the groom). This implied inclusion of the person's language takes off the hard edge of the simple monosyllable.

But you can do better, and you should. You will add an informative sentence to the basic acknowledgment (*Yes, I am*) that allows the conversation to be developed in a new direction. For example, you might add, "We went to Washington State when we were undergrads. We were both interested in drama." This advances the theme of the friendly intent and also introduces free information.

Free information means that you have introduced new potential topics that could now be addressed. You have already exhausted the issue of whether you are or are not a friend of the groom. Yes or no questions have a way of not leading anywhere without further questioning. Your responsiveness, your willingness to offer these encouraging bits of information, will be read as a courteous and encouraging answer and is socially appropriate. (More on chitchat in "Smooth Small Talk.")

Back in our session I would pose simple questions for Leo: "Leo, did you drive here today?" Leo would usually just say "Yeah" and look away. I asked him to change that to "Yes, I did," and led him through a number of simple questions that allowed him to practice this more polite response, using both yes and no answers.

Is it raining today? "No, it isn't."

Was the traffic bad this morning? "Yes, it was."

Did your dog come with you? "No, he didn't."

Notice that Leo has to mirror the language of his partner for this to work. But this was simple work compared to the next step, which asked him to be even more forthcoming about his life.

I asked Leo to append a full sentence to this response to be even more forthcoming with "free information".

Do you leave your dog in the house all day?
"No, I don't. I have a dog walker take him to the park in the afternoon."

Is that a new haircut? "Yes, it is. My mom said I was looking scruffy."

Can you see how the conversational opportunity blooms when you open these personal doors to your life and how the person becomes so much more approachable? Having been so guarded for so much of his life, this step was especially painful for Leo. Although we practiced this several times, when I asked him if he was trying this outside the office, he said "Yeah" and looked away. Changing habits takes a lot of work.

What If You Don't Want to Encourage Conversation?

There are people out there whom you do *not* want to encourage. There are drunks, deadbeats, and damn fools. With these people the abrupt and dismissive "yes" or "no" may be the wisest response in this situation. Be sure to avoid further eye contact and move toward other people. You are responding—they can't say that you didn't—but you are not encouraging anything more. Teenagers are often experts at this.

Whether it is a business or social situation, it is a good idea to keep your psychological doors open to people and develop the habit of the kindlier response. Try to develop your awareness of your own monosyllabic answers and try to append some phrase that softens the response. So many people complain of conversational difficulties and don't realize that they are the ones slamming the door on people reaching out to them.

I had Leo start by acting as if he were a gracious person. Have you heard the expression, "Fake it till you make it"? Leo had to start with social boot camp. (More about Leo in "How You Look When You Talk.")

Let's consider the other end of the spectrum of graciousness and highest level of social-language usage.

The Incredible Transformational Power of Gracious Language

I will tell you three stories that show the memorable use of language to totally transform or reframe a situation. I hope that they inspire you. Inspiration frequently opens doors to possibilities not previously evident to the individual.

First, a humble example that I invite you to consider: You are calling Customer Service of some huge company and (finally!) get connected to a real human being, who says something like, "X-Y-Z-Corporation-Tina-speaking-how-can-I-help-you." At a somewhat lower rate of speech, I will say, "Oh good morning Tina, this is Carol Fleming in San Francisco, and I really need your help." This has never failed to get me excellent, courteous service. Take a minute to figure out why that might be so. You should come up with three features that would open their hearts and cause them to *want* to help you.

Here's another way you can transform a situation for optimal effectiveness (and courtesy). The scene might be dealing with store clerk and you are thinking thoughts like "Stupid!

Incompetent!" etc. How likely are you to improve the situation if you release this pent-up outrage to the clerk? My guess is that you will just make the situation more fraught with tension and unsatisfying. But what if you consider the thought, "I will do what I can to get the best out of them"? Doesn't this suggest another kind of behavior? One that brings the best out of you? You are becoming part of the solution instead of part of the problem.

Story #1

I ordered clam chowder at an Italian restaurant. The first bite revealed sand in the clams, which was a very unpleasant experience. I told the waiter that I would not eat the soup and why. The waiter gave a spirited denial. Oh no, madam, we are always very careful in rinsing clams. We get all the sand out! (Oh really?!) I insisted that he take the bowl back to the kitchen. The maître d' had observed the conversation and went to the kitchen door. I could see the maître d' having a spirited conversation over the soup bowl with the waiter. As the main course arrived, the maître d' came to our table. Was he going to berate me for the returned soup? No. He picked up my hand and brushed the back of it with his lips and said, "Madam, with more customers like you, we will become a better restaurant."

How simple! How elegant! With that one comment, he completely rinsed the sand out of the dining experience and made me feel great. Can you see why this has become my favorite Italian restaurant?

Story #2

This incident takes place on a crowded San Francisco Municipal bus. Most of the riders were made aware of a rather loud and very grimy older woman sitting in the middle of one of the benches at the front of the bus. She shouted out commentaries with surly reproach and to no apparent companion.

She was eager to debate anyone who innocently met her eyes. We quickly learned to keep our eyes down whenever she surveyed the rest of the riders. Here was a loose cannon.

At Geary Street, a group of three young men got on the bus and stood in the front aisle holding onto the overhead straps. One of them was black, and he stood in front of the woman. Before long as the bus became more crowded, we all heard one more yell from the woman: "Get your black ass out of my face!"

My, my, didn't the bus get quiet. People froze with their eyes wide open. I swear we all stopped breathing, because I heard all conversations stop. The bus rolled down Van Ness with a load of people looking straight ahead and strangely silent.

I was able to see the young man from my seat. He didn't move except to glance at his companions briefly. Then, with his head hanging down, I saw him shake his head briefly, look up at the ceiling, and turn toward the woman. He slipped into the empty seat beside her, put his arm around her shoulders, and said, "Now, sugar, how come you to talk so mean to me?" (Take a moment or two to consider this scene.)

She responded immediately, as if to an old friend, "I don't know, I just been so cranky all day. I think I got this flu comin' on and I ain't been sleepin' so good." And so they chatted while the rest of us made profound commentary with our eyes, widening and rolling, a nonverbal Greek chorus of amazement and relief. Perhaps they were old friends! At some point the woman must have gotten off the bus and the space beside the young man was empty. When my stop was coming up, I stood in the stairwell in the front of the bus, waiting for the doors to open. I was still profoundly moved by what I had witnessed. As I passed him, I said, "Blessed are the peacemakers." He dropped his face into his hands and whispered, "Lady, you have no idea what that cost me." I stepped off the bus.

Here was a generous, transcendent act that displayed the gracious, the elegant, response to human orneriness. "Now, sugar," he had said. "Now, sugar" (we have a long-standing loving relationship, see. And I know you are really a sweet person). "Why you talk so mean to me?"—this with an arm around her shoulder, looking straight into her eyes, and witnessed by a whole busload of people. What started as an assault on him was instantly transformed into a confession of personal difficulty. This very public act of forgiveness and kindliness—the physical risk the young man took—made transcendent love real, observed, and right in our face, on a Muni bus.

When our angels fly above the gritty meanness of our lives and do something simply splendid, don't we consider our own possibilities for being just a teensy more generous or tolerant? No, I don't know what it cost him. Whatever that cost, a busload of citizens got an unforgettable lesson.

Story #3

I was privileged to hear the contralto Marian Anderson when I was fourteen years old. Anderson presented a solo concert in the (movie) theater of our small town. I had never heard an opera star, certainly, and I don't think I had ever seen a black woman before. I was the first one in the theater, dressed in my Sunday best. I sat in the middle of a front row by myself and waited as others filled in the audience.

Simply put, she was stunning—her body erect, her head held high, kinetic energy ready to spring forth. To see her was to catch your breath and wait to see what she would do. She seemed to flow onto the stage, wearing a long white satin gown. She stopped and turned in the middle of the stage and just froze, her hands clasped in front of her. But her long white satin train continued to wind around her. I didn't know women could look like this, move like this, make you stop breathing. I was ready to believe anything she told me.

Her voice filled that theater so that it reverberated from every surface. It has been called "the voice of America's soul."

Jessye Norman said, "Her voice ... made me think that if the planet Earth could sing, it would sound something like Marian Anderson." Tears just poured down my cheeks.

After the concert, I hid in the velvet curtains until all the grown-ups left her dressing room, and then I knocked on her door. I was trembling, shaken, and teary-eyed. She answered the door and listened to my shaky voice and tribute. She took both of my hands in hers and patted them, saying, "Thank you, my dear. Thank you so much!" She made me feel as if I had done something extraordinary! She taught me all I needed to know about graciousness.

I Wanna Be Articulate!

Jimmy set his goals for our work together. "Like I was sayin', I, uhhh, jus' wanna talk real good. I wanna sound like Tommy Ryan ... oh yeah! I wanna be articulate!"

When Tommy Ryan (his boss) talked, everybody listened. To describe Tommy's speaking you would need all the really good words in speech description: fluent, resonant, melodic, concise, and articulate. There was a long way between Jimmy and Tommy. Jimmy was a young fellow out of the Midwest in his first job. He was athletic, with average grades. Tommy was forty years older, successful, and confident, and was light-years away in culture, poise, and class. Jimmy had chosen an excellent speech model, just like Everest is an excellent mountain to climb.

People who are articulate have a style of speaking that reveals a cultured mind. Their vocabulary is developed, and they use real words, with few fillers, or empty language (see "Words Fail Me!"). They are concise, using only the language that is pertinent and well-organized (see "Getting Your Point Across"). They speak clearly.

Speech sounds must be sufficiently articulated in the stream of spoken speech to be easily heard. When sounds are omitted, muffled, or distorted, the listener has to make an effort to understand what is said. This can cause problems of understanding and will affect how that person is judged socially.

A Real Problem

The parent tells the housekeeper to pick up the child after school. The housekeeper responds, "I can(t) do that." The housekeeper fully intended to say "I can't," but the parent can only hear "I can" because the /T/ sound in *can't* was not articulated. Unclear speech can have serious consequences.

The Judgment

Speak like Jimmy and people assume a lower-class background, a poor education, limited intelligence, and no polish. You may not get the chance to show what you can do when your first impression is made with sloppy speech.

Mumbling

People frequently use the word "mumble" (or "sloppy") to indicate that they are not producing speech sounds or words clearly. Are you frequently asked to repeat what you have just said? That's a clue.

The tendency to mumble may be associated with speaking too fast or too softly. Please see "Fast Talkers" and "Soft Talkers" for those issues. Let us focus on speech clarity here. I will discuss some of the more general problems that are actually pretty easy to address once you become aware of them. And that is the problem right there. In your mind, you *are* saying the words that you intend (like the housekeeper who said can['t]), but your mouth is only forming a part of that message with sufficient energy or confidence to be heard. The difference between "can" and "can't" seems small, until you consider the consequences of that child not being picked up after school.

Substandard Usage

There is a lot of variation in how words are pronounced. There are differences due to physical characteristics, language background, and the intention of the speaker, the context, etc.—variations that we don't even notice because they don't make a difference in conveying meaning. But some variations (or simplifications) are noted and characterized as substandard.

For example, how do you say the word "our"? It should be pronounced just like the word "hour," but many people say "are" (like /r/) instead. (*That's are car.*) Contrast that with *That's (h)our house.*

It is the frequency and consistency of such small details of articulation that attract notice as substandard speech. These details have to be specifically identified to begin the process of change. Perhaps your work with the Evaluation part of this book has yielded this information. Following is a detailed description of how you might proceed to learn a new pronunciation, using the example of "our."

The general practice procedure described here is an effective approach to most speech sound change and can be used for other problems detailed later in this section.

Say "are" and "hour" as described above, and concentrate on the difference in your mouth. Try to describe to yourself what you are doing in your mouth to make these two words sound differently. Are you feeling some movement in your lips and tongue when you say "hour/our" that you don't notice in the "are"? Try the following sentences, contrasting the two words:

> We *are* going to *our* house.
>
> The people in *our* company *are* satisfied.
>
> What *are* you doing in *our* shop?
>
> What *are our* options?

That last one is a mouthful, isn't it? If this pronunciation of "our" feels strange in your mouth, it means that you are probably used to substituting "are" instead.

You could make up a list of ways that you frequently use "our" (our house, our problem, our chance, our family, our gripe, etc.) and say these combinations slowly, keeping the *our* sounding like *hour*.

Add some words in front of the *our* now, making more complete phrases like:

> Come to our house.
>
> What's our problem?
>
> This is our chance.
>
> That will work with our family.
>
> That's our gripe!

The following sentences (specifically the second question) were a graduating milestone for Jimmy: "Is it over? Or are our options open?" At first, it was all Jimmie could do just to read these three words aloud moving his finger from one word to the next—"or ... are ... our"—eyes wide open in alarm. "Or ... are ... our" would be his tongue twister for the week; he had to do many careful, accurate repetitions of this combination with cautious inclusion of new vocabulary to make a complete phrase. "Do the kids need shots? Or are our kids okay?" "Should we buy some fertilizer? Or are our flowers doing all right?" Or, since Jimmie was in the insurance business, "Do we have to raise our rates? Or are our prices stable?" And, of course, a phone call to me: "Dr. Fleming, can we bill the company for our work? Or are our sessions tax-deductible?" (Yes on both accounts.)

Make up more sentences, proceed slowly, and do lots of careful repetitions every day for a week or so. An extremely effective way of rapid learning is to leave a practice session on your voice mail from another telephone. Then you can listen to it later; do this for a couple of weeks and you'll probably have the problem solved.

Another example of common misusage is the "ek" error: Do you "ekscape" or "escape"? If you "ekscape" you probably also drink "ekspresso," "ek cetera." Here is the correct pronunciation: *es*cape, *es*presso, and *et* cetera. Use the practice plan described for "our" to address this problem.

Here are two final examples: Are libraries important enough to say the word right? "Li(*brer*)ry." Instead, we commonly hear "li*berry*." I engaged a number of people in conversation at a local library last week and found ways to elicit the word "library" from them. The librarians actually said "library," and most everyone else said "liberry." Nonetheless, you can be sure that someone like Tommy Ryan would never say "liberry."

I want you to say the word "nucleus." Nu-cl*ee*-us, right? Now try "nu-cle-ar." (Nu-cle-us/ nu-cle-ar; nu-cle-us/ nu-cle-ar.) Thank you.

Now put the word in some sentences. *(We need to develop nuclear energy. Are you afraid of a nuclear bomb?)* Did you discover that you wanted to say "nuculor" instead? I suspect that some politicians do use this form intentionally to send a social-class message (i.e., wanting to appeal to the working class). In this case, as in the case of the dropped /g/, the usage is intentional and political. Otherwise, it simply sounds uneducated.

Omitted Speech Sounds

To begin with, when we talk about speech sounds, we are not talking about how words are spelled, but how sounds—consonants and vowels—are pronounced in a word. I find that most people have become visually oriented. It is very hard for them to separate how a word looks on the page from how it sounds in the ear. I frequently teach the International Phonetic

Alphabet, a system of phonetic notation that requires focus on the spoken sounds alone. There are several sources on the Internet for speech sounds that may help you understand how phonetics work and the important difference between spelling and speaking. In this section, I will mention some speaking difficulties of the average American speaker. Foreign-born speakers have another set of issues for the most part. Only some of the common errors can be described in print with any confidence on my part.

The articulate person is easy to understand because the necessary speech sounds are made easy to hear. (Note: you can also be hypercorrect when you exaggerate the speech sounds.)

Say the following sentence out loud and record it. Try to say the sentence as you normally would pronounce it. "I was only going to tell him that it was already gone." If I listened to your spoken sentence, I wonder if I would have heard the /l/ sound in the words "only" and "already." Some people will say "on'y" and "a'ready," leaving the /l/ articulation out completely. Typically they are perfectly capable of using a good /l/ sound (leaf, yellow, etc.). It's just in certain words that they have picked up this pronunciation. If you call it to their attention, they will be astonished.

Were you surprised? Did you deliberately put an /l/ in the word and it felt weird? Then we're talking about you. Follow the steps suggested previously for speech change.

The "T" at the End of a Word

The biggest culprit in the "omitted sounds" department is the articulation of the final /t/ sound in words, especially when it is grouped with other consonants. Remember "I can('t) do that"? That /t/ was between an /n/ and a /d/ in the sequence of sounds. Say it slowly yourself. Isn't it interesting that all three speech sounds involve the tip of the tongue? Do you suppose that could explain why it is a difficult combination for the housekeeper?

How do we make that /T/ in the first place? We stop the flow of air abruptly in our mouth with the tongue right behind the teeth. We then release that pent-up air against the back of the front teeth, and there's your /t/. In the case of "can't do," we would have to stop the voice flow of the /n/ abruptly with the tongue behind the teeth in the /t/ place and then release that pressure in the form of the /d/ of the word "do." We *will* hear the /t/ sound with just that abrupt stoppage of voice followed by the explosive /d/ sound. If the /n/ just flows into the /d/, there's no perceived /t/, and the impact on the meaning of this particular phrase is huge. And you thought speech was simple! Ha!

Jimmy would pronounce the words "it was" with an abrupt stoppage in his throat for a /t/. You learned about this habit in "Staccato Talkers." Maybe you do the same thing. Try it. Feel that catch in your throat? If so, it may be that you are making a lot of your /t/'s in your throat instead of producing them in the front of your face, where all good little speech sounds are made.

Put the /t/ in "it" at the front of the word "was," but don't make a big aspiration (air sound); just say "twas." *Itwas*. Yes, that is correct. That /t/ was clearly present and part of the flow of your air and voice, so it will get out into the world instead of sliding down your throat. This simple practice of putting the sound up behind the teeth rather than down in your throat will make a world of difference in your speaking clarity.

Listen to a recording of yourself focusing on your production of /t/ at the end of words. Can you really hear the /t/ or do you hear yourself faking it in your throat? It will be easy to fool you, because we tend to hear what we expect to hear. Deliberately search for evidence of the /t/ sound being produced in the front of your mouth.

Now do the same kind of focused listening to someone whose speech you admire for clarity, your Tommy Ryan. What about those /t/'s? Just this focus of attention will help you become aware of your habit, which is the first step in improving your speech clarity.

Dropping the "G"

In the same sentence used in the previous example, notice what happens with "going to." Did it come out as "gonna"? If so, I am not surprised. Actually, you are not really "dropping" a /g/; you are substituting an /n/ sound for an /ng/ (and omitting the /t/). The /n/ is made with the tongue pressed up behind your front teeth while the back of the tongue comes up to close off the mouth when making the /ng/ sound. Just to assure yourself that you do know how to make this sound, say "sing" or "ring" or "wrong." You might alternate between the two sounds (/n/ and /ng/) to feel your tongue moving so differently. Say "run" and then "rung." Feel it? You have no trouble when it's part of a word. It's that "ing" end on a verb that gets you. If you think this is called a present participle, you're right.

This substitution of /n/ for /ng/ is quite common and a normal substitution in casual speech, especially among men attempting to be "regular guys." Think of the politicians I mentioned before who can deliberately adopt a different dialect in order to court the working-class voter, the message "If I talk like you, I am like you and therefore have your interests at heart," making it easier for the voter to identify with that speaker.

It is very useful to be able to turn off this casual style and turn on a more polished level of speaking when appropriate. The problem only comes when you are unaware of your casual usage and its effect on more discriminating ears. It could make a difference to your future. If someone says, "I'm gonna be goin' by the store and pickin' up some soda," you'd know what he meant without a doubt. If you were asked to assess his education and polish, how would he fare?

Linking

Here are suggestions for practicing the *ing* endings. The concept of linking is important here. When you link your words, you let the voice and energy of the end of one word flow into the next. This will be counterintuitive to many of you. Your inner second grader will protest that I am asking you to slur your speech. Well, yes and no. We are practicing liaison (for those of you who have studied French), and it is entirely appropriate when speaking English. Trust me, you actually do this when you are not thinking about it.

Say "sing along" as you normally would, which means you would glide from "sing" right into "along." Say it slowly and *don't break the two words apart*. Try, "I'm putt*ing o*n my coat." Always glide right into the following sound from the *ing* sound. So it should sound like "puttingon." Focus your attention on how it feels in your mouth to glide from the first word to the next. Work on other combinations, such as "going out," "staying there," "writing to," etc. As in all speech correction, start slow and simple, and build speed and complexity through careful repetitions.

After you have repeated these combinations several times, do them wrong on purpose just to become aware of the contrast in your articulation. This is very helpful in raising your awareness of the incorrect pronunciation.

Casual Form	Correct Form
wantin'	wanting
I'm wantin	I'm wanting
I'm wantin to go.	I'm wanting to go.

Repeat the correct form three times, and then go back and forth between the correct and incorrect versions.

Put your word together with other words that might naturally follow it in a sentence:

> *wanting a drink*
>
> *wanting to go*
>
> *wanting some time*
>
> *wanting more time*

It should sound like this: *Wantinga, wantingto, wantingsome, wantingmore.*

Think about the verbs you are likely to use the most in the course of your work, and use them for your practice (calling, asking, phoning, talking, helping, driving, etc.).

Some Small Details

Jimmy had a problem with the words "the" and "a." "Good heavens!" you say. "Surely everybody can say 'the' and 'a.'" Not so fast. There are a few tricky aspects over which even you might stumble. For example, when reading something out loud, many adults tend to pronounce the word "a" as if it were the name of the letter A. So they will report that "there is A tendency for A new customer to ask for A reduction of A fee." They sound like second graders or a mechanically produced voice. The word is properly pronounced "uh." You do this when you talk naturally. There's just something about oral reading that brings out the latent second grader in you. But you really don't want this to happen in front of the board of directors.

It may have escaped your attention that the word "the" has two pronunciations depending upon the nature of the word that follows. If the next word begins with a vowel, you should use the pronunciation "thee"—thee apple, thee olive, thee office. If it begins with a consonant, "thuh" is used—thuh banana, thuh car, thuh girl. Most people do this naturally, but every once in a while somebody misses the lesson. Of course, nobody ever thinks to teach a foreign-born person this principle.

Improving Articulation

In general, your speech is going to be clearer if you do three things:

1. Get your mouth to move more.
2. Speak a bit more slowly.
3. Direct the flow of speech energy out the front of your mouth (see the next section, "Fronting").

Watch news announcers of your same gender and notice their facial expressions and the amount of movement in their face. Now speak in the mirror, and notice how much you move your own face. You will do this much more accurately if you could use a video camera to observe your speaking objectively. If you see little movement of your jaw and lips, it is likely that your mumbling will be improved with attention to greater movement patterns. You would be wise to enlist the help of a speech professional at the beginning of this effort to provide appropriate guidance for your particular situation and to keep you motivated to do the necessary work. Use the Internet or the Yellow Pages to find a speech pathologist or a voice coach.

Fronting

Fronting refers to the placement of your speaking energy in the front of your mouth instead of the back of your throat. When you speak from the back, it affects your ability to project, as well as the brightness of speech and distinctness of articulation. Vocal vitality and resonance in the front of the face makes a brighter tone that carries. Take a look at "Raspy Talkers" for some exercise material that will help you focus your speaking energy in the front.

Add some chewing jaw movement. Pretend to chew while making sounds like "yum yum yum yum." Keep the feeling of forwardness in the mouth. You are creating sensation patterns in your speech mechanism that are similar to the change you want in your speaking. In this exercise, your jaw moves, you feel vibration in front, and the voice is steady throughout the exercise (not waxing and waning).

Go from "yum yum" into the sentences "One alone to be my own," "Willows bend in the wind," and "People eat sweet peaches at the beach." Try to keep that greater movement of the jaw as you go into real words. Put yourself in front of a mirror to see how you do.

Feel the speech sounds in the front of your mouth and let the voice flow unbroken from beginning to end. (It helps if you put the palm of your hand across your throat to feel the vibration.) Contrast this feeling with a sentence that you will feel in the back of the throat: "It requires raw courage for George to go to church." Now say, "Willows bend in the wind," which has a lot of speech sounds that are made in the front of your mouth. Repeat these sentences in tandem, just to raise your awareness of the difference in the sensations in your mouth. Try recording the sentences so you can hear how they sound.

After you have repeated your "front" sentence (one alone, willows, sweet peaches), say a short simple sentence of your own, such as "I work in this building," "It's a lovely day," or "It's nice to meet you." At first, you will probably do so in your usual style of speaking, of course. Try to get your sentence to feel like your front practice sentence with your speaking energy more forward in your mouth. Alternate the two sentences with this in mind. Your ability to get the new sentences to feel like your practice sentence is the central issue here.

We start practicing with artificial exercises so you're not distracted by the personal reality of your own language. Your brain and mouth need to become accustomed to the new sound and feel of words before you can transfer the learning to your own speaking. Patience!

Read written materials (e.g., plays, newspaper columns, etc.) to consciously practice the frontal focus. Use only short paragraphs and patiently repeat the same material for mastery of your goal. If you select a longer piece, you are likely to lose focus and just speak in your usual style.

Practice new habits with selected words, phrases, and sentences appropriate for your work or life. Get used to what it feels like when you sound the way you want, and record it frequently so you can track your progress. In the beginning, you have to pay attention to both how and what you're saying. Start with one situation, one person to practice with— something safe where it's okay to trip up (strangers, friends, etc.). Work up gradually, selectively, and be resolute about regular practice.

Go back to parts of this program that focus on the problems you want to address. If, when you're practicing, the new habit stops feeling strange, record it to make sure you haven't lapsed into old habits. Of course, eventually this will mean you've achieved the goal. Morning and midday practice are more effective. Don't practice while driving or watching TV— you must have your wits about you to establish new speaking behavior. Adhere to a serious practice schedule, thirty to forty-five minutes a day.

Speech patterns aren't changed by just reading out loud or by intellectual understanding. They are changed by persistence. (You see how I persist in telling you this?)

CHAPTER 5

Unifying Your **Verbal and Nonverbal** Messages

"I told you I love you," he says, his face buried in the newspaper and his voice absolutely flat. This is what is known as a mixed message, and you don't know what to believe. You probably *want* to believe the words—the content of the message—but somehow it is just not ringing true.

People read each other in rather complex ways, and we use more than just words to figure out meaning. As it happens, *what* somebody says—the actual words—carries only a small component of the emotional information, while tone of voice accounts for much more of the impact. But the nonverbal parts, the physical part of facial expression and body language, are registered even more powerfully and can take command of the message. This is how we work our way through sarcasm, noting the difference between tone of voice and the words. And if we're still not sure, we look at the speaker for more information.

If you are among the savvy, you've been paying attention to the subtleties of vocal intonation and to the fleeting microgestures (expressions) on faces. But many of us have had intense and exclusive concern with verbal language and have dismissed the sound and the look of speaking as being peripheral rather than central to communication. In my experience, this is more true of men than women. If you are simply exchanging pure information, words work just fine: how to run the office copy machine, monthly cash flow statements, etc.—information that can just as well be written. But it does not work in human relations when you're actually talking with people like your sweetheart, your employee (or boss), or the clerk at the bank.

The tonal and visual aspects of speaking are features that we share with our fellow primates. They are basic and important parts of our face-to-face communication—have been for thousands of years—and must not be ignored. Their contribution to meaning is immediate and visceral in contrast to the processing of abstract symbols such as numbers and words. All of these sources of information—the verbal, vocal, and physical—come together to form a reality that is more than the sum of its parts and actually constitute the personality of the individual. The majority of people are very good at reading the three channels of human communication, as long as we're talking about *other* people. We usually don't know what we're sending out to others. We're pretty good about the verbal part, the words, but our tonalities and expressions leak information of which we may or may not be aware. This leakage may give the lie to your words. And when these three forms of communication don't add up, you are sending out a mixed message that makes others uneasy. You lose credibility.

There's a high price to pay for mixed messages. Carl and his brand-new bride came from Germany about forty years ago. They settled, built a manufacturing business in the Bay Area, employed a good many people, and made a solid, reputable product. The time had come when Carl was ready to sell the business, retire, and then spend some serious time with his grandchildren.

Then he got sued for three million dollars. "Breach of contract," they said. A man of fierce pride and honor, Carl was outraged. When his attorney saw how much of Carl's emotional reaction would color his testimony, Carl was sent to me.

We filmed the initial run-through of his testimony using questions the attorney had supplied. From the video, it became immediately apparent why he was in my office: his jaw became immovable, the brow lowered, and the eyes, a steely blue, became a squint. He gave terse responses in a flat voice and his nostrils quivered in disdain. He was totally focused on accuracy and unaware of emotional message. Were I to cast a WWII movie, I would surely have Carl as a Nazi officer. I didn't tell him that, of course.

What I did do was have him tell me about his grandchildren. His face opened, he chuckled and sparkled, he became fluent and jolly, and you could just see the lederhosen and hear the oompah band. Here was a man you would be happy to listen to. And believe. His description of his business success was equally pleasant and easy to listen to.

We clearly needed more of this contented person on the witness stand. This aspect of his personality was just as genuine as his embittered self.

I showed Carl the videotape of the two conversations, and he could clearly see the difference in impact. I would turn off the sound so he could just appreciate the effect of his facial expressions. Getting him to go over his testimony with a different emotional "set" was a challenge for Carl. He had felt that he should act out his indignation for the jury. With enough repetitions of the taping, Carl started to giggle at some of his mannerisms, and he became more open to change.

Carl needed to know that his sense of personal insult and resentment of the plaintiff did not have to be acted out in court when he was being asked to describe business practice and contracts. Indeed, it detracted from it. Carl was proud of his accomplishments; he needed to sound like that. He had proceeded in good faith; he needed to look like it.

You can't talk reasonably, openly, and honestly and look and sound truculent and guarded. People will surely respond to the emotional display over the rational content. Use your head and get aligned with other feelings that are equally valid and more in tune with your main message.

Notice how much trouble is engendered when people let extraneous emotion intrude on otherwise straightforward or business communications. We see it all the time in the workplace when people bring personal issues to the job where they have no place. When you must work with the public, there will be many times that you will have to overlook or submerge personal insult for the greater good of your employer or the future of the particular relationship. You have a choice here.

In the next section, you'll learn how to unify your nonverbal messages, or body language, with both the sound of your voice and your words. When all three of these elements of communication are in sync, your message will come across clearly, and you'll seem much more professional, reliable, and impressive. (P.S. Carl settled out of court, but he told me that our work together helped him really see how we are expert at reading the look and the sound of each other. A new world of meaning was revealed.)

Carrying Yourself with Confidence

My friend Leah can buy a dress for a dollar at a garage sale. And when she wears that dollar dress, it's easy to imagine her on the cover of *Vogue* magazine. Anything looks great when Leah wears it because she carries herself gracefully.

Some of you may be very skilled at reading the carriage of people the minute you see them. There's a certain military feel about this man, something defeated in this woman, something provocative about that girl, or something about that person that's a little scary. If you're like most people, you're not particularly good at identifying which specific cues you're interpreting; it's "just a feeling" you get. You are responding to cues both obvious and subtle. Let's examine some of these nonverbal cues to put you in a better position to improve your own impact on others.

How You Carry Yourself

You probably make thoughtful choices when you dress yourself, but it is your posture that will actually determine how well you look in your wardrobe. Posture is also used to determine your attitude. If you picture persons of power and achievement, you probably imagine these people with an upright carriage and composed movement pattern. Distortions of the body alignment, as when you make haste and get frantic, destroy any semblance of composure. You need to become aware of any extraneous movement, fiddling or self-touching, that draw attention to itself. You don't make these movements intentionally, so getting aware is step number one.

Cynthia—thirty-two, mother of three—was sent to me by her boss in a property management firm to increase her professionalism and credibility. They were concerned about "demeanor and emotional expressiveness." Cyn had no idea what kind of behaviors they were talking about. She told me she always tried to be friendly and very encouraging with people. I had her tell me about the long-range plans of her company while I video-recorded her. It did not take her long to see on the videotape the very mannerisms that concerned her boss. She constantly cocked her head to one side and used lots of facial expressions. This gave her a childlike appearance and demeanor that detracted from her professionalism. I'll bet you've noticed people who do not hold their heads in an upright fashion. You may have noticed the hang-dog posture, the bobble-head-doll nodding, and the cocked-to-one-shoulder coquette.

Head carriage is a profound communicator of attitude, and it is the primary indicator of dignity. Would you, like Cyn, like to appear more mature and dignified? All it takes is a hardcover book as a feedback device to help you get in control of your head movement.

Find a hardcover book (just slightly bigger than your head). Stand in front of a mirror and balance the book on top of your head. I have a particularly beat-up book with a textured cover that I offer for this purpose in my office. If you are like Cyn, just getting that book to stay put is the first challenge. You have to learn how to hold your head still enough for the book to stay flat and put. Give your body the time it takes to learn this posture. Pay attention to what you are doing with the rest of your body that allows the book to stabilize. This is what you are trying to learn.

Now stretch your body up, lengthening your neck, keeping your shoulders down and relaxed. Don't just stick your chin up. Increase the distance between your ears and shoulders. Watch yourself in the mirror so you don't do something weird with your posture. You are now erect and looking proud.

Turn your head slowly from side to side, keeping the chin line even. Take a few steps, side to side, front to back, keeping the head even and the book flat. Now, try walking around maintaining your posture. Try to have some normal arm swing. Yes, I know it will feel funny at first, but with enough practice, it will start to feel natural. And, yes, the book will fall to the floor a number of times as you learn these new smooth coordinations. It's okay.

Sit and talk on the phone with a friend, and try to keep the book balanced. You will probably discover that you do a lot of head bobbing when you talk, because the darned book will slide off your head often. Start with short and easy conversations so you can have some attention to devote to your head control.

I hope you are willing to spend some time on these conversations because this is an excellent "real" communication situation where you'll be able to learn to control your nonverbal mannerisms as you are actually speaking to a person.

When you think you've gotten the feel of it, take the book off your head and see if you can maintain the posture from body memory. Have a mirror positioned so you can monitor your head control. Make it a practice for several days to put the book on and off as you converse on the phone. I am assuming that you have a private room or a tolerant workplace in which to do this! Soon you'll just have to think "book" to straighten up when you want to.

Start noticing how other people hold their heads. You'll find that you will form an opinion of their sense of personal worth, pride, health, and vigor by their head carriage. Notice how they carry their bodies in space, and ask yourself if a book would stand a chance.

Posture.

People prefer a walking pattern that has the arms close to the body and the legs close under the body. As kids, we used to play "Clem Kadiddlehopper" and walk like we were staggering over deep furrows with our legs spread out and our arms flailing away at the side. Perhaps you've seen this pattern out on our city sidewalks, but this stance doesn't do well in the workplace. Your arms should swing naturally by your side when you walk and your hands should just graze your body as they pass. If you have a chance to examine your foot plant, see how far apart you tend to carry your legs. Keep your feet no more than eight inches apart as you walk, and you'll be more likely to develop a graceful, pleasing gait.

As you walk, you'll also want to avoid lifting yourself up on the balls of your feet as you step forward, as that results in a bouncy step that detracts from your carriage of maturity. Try balancing that book on your head as you walk and you will learn rapidly if you have too much movement in your stance.

Do you notice the people who are hunched over with their heads stuck out like turtles? They are carrying their weight forward, distorting their carriage to get wherever they're going. They look like they're constantly *striving* and not assured in their carriage. I sure hope that's not you. Start with the book-balancing exercise described above. We're going to weave a fantasy around that posture.

Pretend you have a crown on your head and a long ermine cloak on your shoulders. Walk for some distance with this image. This keeps your head up (to balance the crown) and your shoulders back (from the weight of the cape). If you can have someone videotape you with this posture, all the better—you will not believe how good you look. This posture speaks assured self-possession. It just has to be seen to be believed. Cyn paraded up and down the hall in front of my office with her "crown" and "cloak" in mind. She felt silly as the dickens. But I could record her stride and was able to show her a before and after. She really liked what she saw and was willing to do the systematic practice to make it easy and natural.

The best way to practice a new movement pattern is to select certain specific occasions where you will be able to use the pattern in your daily life. For example, Cyn decided she would use her regal posture whenever she walked into a facility, went to the office copier, walked down the hallway to the restroom, etc. As she became more comfortable, she added more situations where she was mindful of her carriage. Soon it became more automatic for her. It won't be long before she will be able to buy a dollar dress from the neighborhood garage sale and be able to carry it off with style.

How You Look When You Talk

We are extraordinarily skilled in interpreting the expressive movements of the face. Notice that even when you are able to hear speakers with no difficulty you still prefer to observe their face while they speak. You not only pick up more information about speech production on the face, but you are getting a lot of emotional and attitudinal information. Have you ever wondered what other people see when they watch your face? It is not what you see in the mirror. Being videotaped during conversation is one of the only ways you can catch your expressive patterns and understand what other people are observing.

Remember Cynthia in the last chapter? In addition to cocking her head to one side in a distracting manner, she kept her face in fairly constant movement when she spoke. She would widen her eyes and distort her face in other ways as part of her emotional expressiveness. The senior staff did not want excessive "emotional expressiveness" on the job, they told me, but not one of them was able (or willing) to tell Cyn exactly what she was doing that was detracting from her presentations. In my view her variable expressions and attitudes immediately identified her as the encouraging mother or elementary school teacher, and not the vice president of the corporation. Raising her eyebrows repeatedly while she spoke led to additional and prominent forehead wrinkling. I prescribed "Scotch Tape therapy."

Removing a roll of tape from my desk drawer, I proceeded to place several strips of tape diagonally on Cyn's forehead (much to her amusement). I asked her some questions and encouraged her to chat with me. As she warmed to her topic, she started raising her eyebrows and furrowing her brow. The presence of the tape made her instantly aware of doing so. Cyn was wide-eyed as she began to understand how much she moved her eyebrows. Repeated experiences of this allowed her to learn how to recognize, anticipate, and squelch the movement pattern. The difference in her perceived dignity was marked. She now looked composed and centered. I wish you could have seen her face when she looked at the difference in her before and after videos! (Yes, her eyebrows shot up!)

A real conversation in front of a video camera will tell you what you need to know about your facial expressiveness. It will capture what a mirror never can. If you can organize several buddies to make this videotape with you, you will be more likely to capture the genuine expressions you use in real conversation.

Bruce, a young man in his late twenties, told me that some acquaintances had described him as aloof and condescending when he spoke to people. Bruce said that he certainly didn't feel that way about people; in truth, he was desperate for socialization. There had to be something about the way he talked that was making him an unlikeable fellow. He was ready to do something about it, if he could only figure out what "it" was! I recorded our conversation, of course, to see if there was anything in his intonation patterns or words that would help us understand this reaction. I also turned on the video camera that sits beside me in my office. We found our answer in the camera.

As Bruce got involved in his conversation, his head started tilting back so that he ended up literally "looking down his nose" at this listener. This was why he was perceived as snooty. By the end of the session, we even figured out why he did this: he was trying to see clearly. Bruce wore trifocal eyeglasses that he was adjusting with head tilting, and he had really bushy eyebrows that hung over his eyelids. He was also lifting his head to avoid the interference. Solvable problems! Bruce had his eyebrows trimmed and his glasses adjusted, and with a little conscious practice—because habits may persist even when the original causes are removed—he looked like the normal, approachable guy he wanted to be.

Leo, a single man in his mid-thirties, was trying to figure out the many social failures he had had in his life. On the phone his voice was quite measured, quiet, and rather flat in intonation. He wanted a consultation because he was utterly baffled by his inability to get employed at a level of his academic preparation. He had made encouraging progress through a very prominent graduate school with excellent grades and an impressive degree. He interviewed for numerous positions and was never chosen. He was taking part-time jobs more suited for a less educated person. Leo could not understand why his promising career track had just fizzled out. His first reaction had always been to blame someone else for his problems, but after years had gone by, even he was getting suspicious of this conclusion.

As soon as Leo sat down in my office for our interview, I started the video camera. After just a minute of recording, I played the tape for Leo, making no comment. He watched for a while, looked up at me, and said, "I look like a serial killer." We sat in silence for quite a while as we pondered the impact of this revelation.

The flat affect in his voice, the unmoving face with little blinking, was definitely unsettling. Indeed I was struggling to find kindly words to tell him of this impact when he saved me by saying it himself. (People are so much more willing to accept as insight what they hate to learn through critique.)

It will probably come as no surprise that Leo had few acquaintances and no group activities. Sitting home alone or in front of a TV or computer (as he had always done) does nothing for communication or social skills building in the real world. What to do? Was his "serial killer" demeanor the result of limited social exposure—or the cause? Where does one begin?

There needs to be a social milieu in which to learn and practice new behaviors, so I tried to encourage Lee to get involved in something that he genuinely cared about. Sharing concerns was a good way to meet like-minded people and form friendships. The last I heard, he was trying to figure out how to get his way in his homeowners' association. He is on the first rung of learning about diplomacy and consideration. But at least he is trying.

Be aware that most people will be very awkward in giving feedback. They may tell you the result ("you seem snooty") rather than *why* they get the impression ("you are literally looking down your nose at me"). They will probably not even know why they get the impression that they do, but you could ask, "If you have any idea why people think that, I'd sure like to know about it."

We need to try to stay open and receptive to feedback that people offer. Bruce's follow-up on the feedback from his friends was a smart and life-changing move. Leo appeared to accept that his demeanor was the reason he had been looking for to make sense of his life. That information seemed to be enough for him.

What you see in the mirror is not what other people see. Be open for information.

Making Eye Contact

You are probably uncomfortable talking to shifty-eyed folks, the ones who do not look at you when you are talking (or listening) to them. Eye contact is eloquent in several situations that really matter to most people:

Interaction: Conversation is a cooperative joint interaction that requires careful regard of the partner in order to monitor communication success, emotional responses, and to signal turn-taking. The meeting of eyes during the back-and-forth of speaking is essential for this monitoring and sense of relationship and crucial for building trust ("Look me in the eye and say that!").

Intimidation: When we stare fixedly at someone, with brows somewhat lowered, a profound nonverbal warning is being sent ("You are a problem. Stop it!"). Then we look away and do not look back at the person. You have just sent the message, "You are beneath notice! You are being shunned!" We are not the only primate that uses direct eye contact in order to intimidate. Spend some time at the zoo and observe how monkeys and apes signal and read each other.

Intimacy: You can spot the lovers in the café. They gaze into each other's eyes without blinking, their faces relaxed, being maximally receptive to their partner. They simply cannot pull their eyes away from each other. Notice how the pupils of their eyes have widened. ("Drink to me only with thine eyes and I will pledge with mine.") This is maximum interest and adoration, folks. You'll know it when you see it. Not a good time to interrupt.

These emotional communications are profound and deeply rooted in our biological psyche. Eye contact is not trivial or incidental. If people complain that you don't give them eye contact during interaction, treat this feedback as important information.

If your habit is to avert your eyes from other people, you'll want to change this habit with some small but attainable goals. Start by just glancing at people's eyes as you pass them in the street or hall. In other words, just get your eyes off of the sidewalk and into people's faces. If necessary, you can also look at their glasses or ears to give the impression of eye contact. (This was one of the first suggestions I gave to Leo.)

You can practice at home by "talking" to portrait photographs, making sure to speak to their eyes. Try to carry over this behavior when you talk to a neutral ear like the clerk in the drugstore. Keep practicing with different people to build the habit. Short but frequent glances in a relaxed manner are all that is needed.

Important: Be aware that different cultures can have very different standards and interpretations of eye contact. That person who doesn't make direct eye contact with you may be demonstrating great deference or respect in his/her culture. You might want to look into it before you judge them as "evasive."

Never forget that prolonged eye contact can be misunderstood. While you may be simply looking in amazement at some person, your gaze may well be interpreted as either unwanted interest or hostility. ("What are you looking at!") These judgments are made very fast. What to do? Just break your gaze immediately and look away to forestall misinterpretation. It happens.

Showing Your Interest

Have you ever received poor marks in listening in a performance review or in an emotional squabble? You may, in fact, be an adequate listener (i.e., you may be hearing what people are saying), but you are not being *perceived* as listening.

Let me help you *look* as if you are listening. It is an active behavior that communicates to others that you are giving them your attention and involvement.

Stop what you are doing—reading, filing, writing, flower arranging, etc.—when you are spoken to. The faster you stop, the more respect you are paying to the speaker. The message is that they are more important than whatever you are doing. Making them wait until you are good and ready to attend to them gives the reverse message. We've all had this experience with personnel in department stores and restaurants.

If you cannot stop because you are engaged in an important ongoing task when someone approaches you, you might say, "I'll be with you in just a moment," as you finish with some detail. People will usually understand this.

Look at the person speaking. There is no better way to give yourself—your regard, your attention, your time, your receptivity—than with your eyes. To stay glued to the computer monitor, newspaper, or slot machine while another speaks is a clear sign of relative lack of importance. Your looking at the person is the signal he is waiting for.

If you need to visually monitor something important, you can mention it: "My little one is on her trike outside and I need to keep an eye on her ..."

Lean toward them. A slight inclination of the head or body is a signal of approval. You are trying to get closer to the speaker, to reduce the distance. This is perceived as listening. You may think of "listing" as in the tilting of a boat.

Nod your head occasionally as the person speaks. This reassures the speaker that you are attending to his message. It signals encouragement of the communication, not necessarily agreement with the message. Too much nodding or interjecting ("yeah, yeah, yeah ...") can be felt as a hurry-up signal and is counterproductive.

Reflect what they've said, at least some part of it, after they've spoken. Remember, we're talking about making people feel heard, not just answering their questions. Do not do a parrotlike repetition, but reflect enough content to confirm that you have not only received but also processed the message. Include the emotional component in your version and the individual will feel deeply heard. An empathic response to a complaining statement could take this form: "Sounds like the new hire is really causing you a problem. I wish I were in a position to help, but I would only step on toes in this case and probably make things worse. How would you feel about talking to HR?" Or you could just say, "Not my job!" Which one sounds better to you?

Do you deal with a troublesome person who keeps repeating the same message? Concentrate on making him feel heard by using the signals we have discussed, and that may well be all that he really wants.

This next paragraph is addressed to men: Do you have ladies in your life that get upset with your apparent lack of listening to their concerns? A word of advice: shut up. Do not try to immediately fix their problem in your matter-of-fact way, but let the lady vent about her upset. Ask pertinent questions, commiserate, find out what solutions have occurred to her, etc. Don't try to move on to solution until she indicates that this is what she wants. Wait to be asked. Some day you'll thank me for telling you this.

Trying to break the ice in a new work environment? You can make a good first impression by making a deliberate effort to pay attention to the concerns and interests of other people. You might make a more or less formal approach to this by starting a mini dossier on various people. For example, write down some details of a person's life for future reference, something that you notice or overhear. If the secretary is late and you hear that her daughter was sick, you make a note of that. If a colleague is going to be in a race of some sort, write it down. If you overhear that a certain deal is in the works, write down a few words on your list. Later on you can inquire, "How's your daughter doing?" or "How did that race turn out?" The individuals will be pleasantly surprised that you paid attention and remembered some detail of their own life, something of significance to them. You will be perceived as a good listener and a thoughtful person. You might actually become one. This is what you want.

Becoming Approachable

Imagine yourself at a networking or social event where you don't know anybody. You tell yourself to go up to someone and start a conversation. But whom should you approach? Think for a moment about what would determine your selection in this situation. I'm guessing that you would try to find someone who looked friendly, nonthreatening, interesting, and ready for contact, i.e., "approachable." But what do people actually *do* to look that way? Answer that, and you'll know what you should be doing yourself.

It is so much easier for you to be the person who is approached rather than the one making the approach. In this section we will consider the various ways that you can increase the likelihood that others will be drawn to you.

There are three words—select, soften, and search—that can guide your nonverbal communication toward easier social contacts and conversation facilitators.

Select

Before you even leave for a social event, select an item of apparel that is a good conversation piece: belt, scarf, handbag shoes, pin, or necktie. A printed T-shirt (in more casual settings) can be a wonderful and easy conversation starter. If people wanted to approach you they could comfortably comment on this article: "I saw that interesting pin in your lapel; isn't that a Rotary pin? My dad was very active in the Sausalito chapter. Do you belong?" "Where did you find that wonderful handbag? That is so clever!" "You ran in the Bay-to-Breakers race? I did it last year. How did you do?" "I was noticing your interesting ring. Is that a jade?" "I see that you have a brochure from the Rose Show; are you interested in roses? I just ordered six new bushes that were recommended at the show." These opening comments can lead to easy exchanges that go beyond the immediate focus. In the first example, you can develop the Rotary or the Sausalito connection, or both.

Notice the items that other people choose that enable conversation, and think about how you could add something like that to your wardrobe selection. You probably have something wonderful that you haven't considered from a conversational viewpoint. Get it out and take it to a party! It just might do all the icebreaking you need.

(Do you know what these interesting articles used to be called? Conversation pieces.)

SOFTEN

S.O.F.T.E.N. is an acronym that summarizes the nonverbal behaviors you should display when you want to make it easy for other people to approach you (from *Making Contact* by Arthur Wassmer).

<u>S</u>mile at people. People need to see warmth and welcome on your face. Let your face register how you would look if you saw somebody you really liked. (Don't overdo it.)

<u>O</u>pen posture. Face people, arms at your side so the body is more or less open (as opposed to being all angles, guarded, or turned away). You want to look unguarded.

<u>F</u>orward lean. When you are speaking or listening, incline your body in the other person's direction. This is a subtle approach signal that communicates listening.

<u>T</u>ouch. The handshake is an especially important ritual of social greeting. People hate bad handshakes! Your hand should be warm and clean, and you should try for a full grip so that the web of your thumb connects with the web of their thumb. Handshaking is the same for ladies and gents. Ask some of your older friends to check out your handshake and let you know if it feels all right.

<u>E</u>yes. You will want to make interactive eye contact (see "Making Eye Contact") with a conversational partner and avoid looking over his shoulder at other people. Social conversations tend to be limited in time, so make that person feel that he is receiving the whole of your attention.

<u>N</u>od. That little nodding of the head indicates that you are paying attention to what the speaker is saying and will encourage him to continue.

You become approachable to the degree that you *soften* your nonverbal message. Think of becoming more like a marshmallow than a sharp corner.

Search

Observe people in social conversation, and notice that their expressions, postures, and the nonverbal signals being sent between them make a difference in how you feel about approaching them for conversation.

You might notice that the person standing alone is the easiest person to approach. To what extent does that person appear to be open for engagement? He is probably hoping that somebody will rescue him and will welcome your self-introduction.

You might also notice that it seems awkward to approach two people who are engaged in face-to-face conversation. Their shoulders are squared with each other, marking an intense conversational relationship. You would be correct to wait until at least one of them has stepped back with one foot so that they've created a space for a third person.

Develop your sensitivity to the different nonverbal cues and subtleties of the various cultures and age groups. Frequently what one culture offers as their most polite behavior can be perceived as rude by another culture. For example, how much space between us do we feel comfortable with? What about physical contact? In this increasingly multicultural world of ours, make it a priority to become aware of these differences. They are actually quite fascinating.

As you start noticing what makes it easy for you to approach a stranger, you will start becoming more aware of your own social signals. Sharp corners or marshmallow? Consider your *select, soften,* and *search* opportunities to maximize your connection cues at the next get-together. I predict you will be amazed at how effective they are in creating social comfort.

How to flirt long-distance.

Here's a practical example of how to use nonverbal cues across distance to signal that you are approachable.

Let's say you see an attractive person on the other side of the room that you would really like to meet. You watch to see if they seem to know anyone that you know; perhaps you can wrangle an introduction. No? Take matters into your own hands—with your eyes.

1. Stare fixedly at the person until they look around and catch you looking at them.

2. Immediately break your gaze and put your head down, as if embarrassed by being caught staring at them.

3. Immediately lift your head and look back with a sort of embarrassed smile ... then look away.

    a. You have just sent a message encouraging them to work their way around the room and come meet you.

    b. They will feel safe approaching you without the usual social supports of introduction, since you have initiated the 'come on'.

    c. Try it. It's great fun.

Short Person, Big Message

If you are a tall person, you may be wondering what this topic is doing in a communication article. If you are short, you know darn well why it's here. You've probably noticed that you seem to be frequently overlooked and underheard, and promotions appear to go to people of stature and power (and research proves it!).

The person of short stature is surely aware of our cultural bias for the taller person. Short = child/weak; tall = adult/ strong; etc. If you don't deal with this successfully, you are possibly facing frustration, lowered self-esteem, a lack of career progression, and sometimes depression.

I want to tell you about the amazing Julie who went from being a speech therapist for a major rehabilitation provider to being the director of all rehabilitation services in the company. Her "problem" was that she was four-eleven and cute as the dickens. But she had three other characteristics in the mix: she was smart, she was focused on her goals, and she assumed responsibility for her impact (demeanor, appearance, and verbal communication).

A deliberate and businesslike demeanor came to her easily, and she learned to act as if she were tall and successful. Let's see if this same program can help you develop your inner tall person.

Nonverbal Communication

Carriage: Posture must be upright, quasi-military. Don't have an inch that you relinquish to gravity. Get feedback about your carriage from friends or a video of you walking normally. Imagine a crown on your head that you hold up proudly (see "Carrying Yourself with Confidence"). Head control is extremely important in establishing a mature, dignified demeanor. Don't we talk about being "levelheaded"? Make even your nodding purposeful.

A person who holds himself up will appear to be confident and adult. Step back a pace from face-to-face interactions with tall persons so you don't distort your posture by craning your neck uncomfortably.

Clothing, another nonverbal cue, can make a huge difference in your physical impact. Fit is crucial here. Do *not* appear in any clothes that are too big for you or ill-fitting in any way; it would really send the message of child-wearing-adult-clothes. If you have any money to spend, spend it on tailoring.

A number of my clients have been so small that they had to shop in children's departments to find anything that fit. The solution to one problem presented another; they seldom find the quality and stylish features of a wardrobe that they require when shopping in the kiddies' department. If at all possible, you would be way ahead by consulting a wardrobe and image expert to help you select colors and styles that complement your personal style, flatter your physique, and set you off as "very well dressed." They also know where you are likely to find suitable choices for your professional presentations. A personal tailor can make the stylish and well-fitted wardrobe you need.

Both men and women should avoid cuffed trousers (or any strong horizontal lines). Ladies, no girly selections with frills or a teenage look. Men, make sure your tie doesn't hang down below your belt.

In most human interactions, the dimensions of your character and self-respect will matter more than physical stature as people get to know you. But your carriage and wardrobe function importantly in first impressions.

Vocal Communication

You may be short, but that doesn't mean that your voice has to sound small. You should have a mature voice with adult intonations. We all know that a high voice is associated with a small body (i.e., a child). Because you are very aware of this, you may try to push your voice down to the very bottom of your range. This just makes you sound desperate, and your voice will not sound good at all.

Use more simple declarative sentences when you talk (see "Using the Simple Declarative Sentence"). Avoid stringing sentences together with conjunctions: "I went to see him and he said he didn't care so I told him the whole story, but ... blah, blah," and on and on. Here's a stronger version: "I went to see him. He said he didn't care. I told him the whole story." The shorter your phrases, the more emphatic your speech will be. Read these two versions out loud to experience the great difference in maturity.

Avoid extreme fluctuation in your intonation where your voice goes sky high or swoops around in great leaps. This sounds childlike and excitable. Keep your cool and have your melodic line contained—not monotone, but contained.

Present yourself as someone in authority, expecting respect. This means a more serious demeanor. Julie's assurance stemmed from her confidence in her training, so she projected professionalism right from the beginning.

Be deliberate in your movement, in your language selection, and especially in your speech rate. Rushing is for those who meet the schedules of other people. Hurried speech is a form of deference, and it is also frequently hard to understand. Do not let events or personalities make you speak rapidly; you need to be "above" such excitation.

Energy and precise articulation reveal commitment to the message. That's why you don't have to "hype it" with empty intensifiers (it's very, very important!). Just the way you say it with deliberate and clear articulation communicates its importance.

Avoid superlatives: "Fantastic! Terrific! Adorable! You were just great! I loved the way you handled that!" These expressions make you sound like an undiscriminating teenager (see "Words Fail Me!"). Exercise a cooler judgment and make your highest praise a little harder to get. Higher standards reveal more mature range of experience.

Demeanor: Pursue graciousness as a characteristic. You want to recognize virtue in subordinates and avoid speaking ill of others. To blame is to claim helplessness, which you do not want. But do defend your leadership turf:

- Do not let yourself be perceived as "cute" or "amusing."
- Do not let yourself be interrupted.
- Do not respond to distractions.

So if you are short, keep your carriage, demeanor, and statements contained (in verbiage, vocabulary, and melody) and you will be perceived as bigger. That's how it works.

CHAPTER 6

Let's Talk
Business!

Do you need to develop your professionalism? Dealing with the public on behalf of a business requires you to conduct yourself in a way that reflects your personal identification with your occupation. You need to understand what being professional means and how you can communicate it.

The three aspects of work behavior that will be considered important to your professionalism are your *expertise*, your *attitudes and standards*, and your *communication skills*. Performance reviews *always* consider communication skills.

Expertise

This word describes what you know or do that has (monetary) value to others. When you "know your stuff," what is the stuff you know? Your stuff may be old or cutting-edge. It may be traditional and well-understood (dentist), or technical (computer architect), or vague (administrative assistant).

No matter what your particular job is, it is important that you be able to articulate what your capability is. *If it is ill-defined, it is hard to sell or defend.* Try to describe what you (can) do to your friends with concrete descriptions of your activities. Their questions may help you realize what you have omitted saying. Practice this so you are fluent as well as accurate.

You also need to mention achievements, milestones, and credentials, which will tell the story of your commitment to your professional development. How do you develop your area of expertise, and how can you demonstrate this?

Attitudes and Standards

This important area is hard to define, but you sure know it when it's not there. Consider these examples:

> a dentist with dirty hands
>
> a psychotherapist who discusses her clients by name in public
>
> a receptionist who makes you feel unwelcome
>
> a salesperson who would much rather giggle with other clerks than spend time with potential customers.

These are all examples of unprofessional behavior. In these cases, the individuals may have a satisfactory level of expertise, but their poor attitudes and standards will be immediately apparent and will scuttle their careers just as fast as any lack of knowledge.

It is not enough to just know your trade. You must discern and develop the necessary people skills to deliver your expertise appropriately and to create the trust and respect from clients and co-workers. You must communicate your character.

Communication Skills

This large area of communication skills offers the most opportunity for personal development, no matter what your line of work. It is the most available kind of training. It is the most transferable training. And it is an important piece of all human relations. That's because this area contains the behaviors that relate your work to the rest of the world. How are people to know these qualities unless they are somehow communicated by you?

Yes, we are talking about public speaking here. And about business/social conversation. And about courtesy. We are talking about ways of organizing information that ensure response, follow-through, confirmation, and retrieval. We are talking about having speech and voice patterns that people hear as mature and responsible.

Are You a Professional Voice User?

Do you teach? Negotiate? Provide direct customer service? Do you have to interview people? Deliver a training program? Counsel students? Do you work with a team? Manage a department? Deliver a sermon? Are you on the phone a lot? Are you a receptionist? Then you are a professional voice user and need to be mindful of the sound of your voice.

If you feel you do not have the communication skills you need in the workplace, the next section can help you lay a sturdy foundation. And if you find you want even more after you've worked through these chapters, you can seek out training that may be available through your company or the resources of your community. Community college courses? Private training companies?

Invest in your communication skills in every way you can. They have a sure return.

Making an Impressive Self-Introduction

Let's say you are at a luncheon, and everybody is supposed to stand up and introduce themselves. You would want to take advantage of this opportunity so that people will see you in a favorable light. You'll want to avoid the mistakes that you've noticed in others. You've seen some people who just lurch into their name (which you cannot hear!) and do not command an ounce of attention (and usually do not get it). They do not put any energy into getting their message out there so that people can actually get to know them. Let's learn from these painful examples so you take maximum benefit from these opportunities.

Here are a few practical tips that will help you be much more effective in getting your self-introduction heard and remembered.

Go into this situation with a *conscious intention* to make yourself easily heard and seen. Be mindful of the size of the room, and try to position yourself so you have most of the people in front of you. Try to not stand in front of a window or a strong light source that will make it hard for people to see you.

Remember that you are not just there as an individual but as a *representative of a company.* As a matter of fact, at that moment in time, you *are* the company. Regardless of your personal reservations, you must project the pride and energy of your business identification. This must override any personal reservations. That's what being a professional means. So check your dread and gotta-get-through-it attitude at the door. This defeatist attitude will most certainly muffle your words and hide your face.

Be mindful of how you get up. As you see your turn is approaching, push your chair back from the table, making sure you've removed the napkin from your lap and that you do not knock over a glass of water, your chair, or your neighbor's briefcase as you get up out of your chair. These little upsets distract others and make you feel foolish. It just takes a moment of thought to spare you an hour of chagrin.

This will be the first time that people will hear your name, so you need to *say it quite deliberately.* A tiny pause before and after your name will help people understand lit clearly. Say it as if it were underlined. For example, "My name is ... *Carol ... Fleming.*" This is even more important if your name is Vassily Grigoriyants or Sachiko Miyashita. The more unusual your name is, the more time you must let it linger in the air, with pauses, to allow the unfamiliar name to register.

Think about what you want to say before you engage your mouth. If I am in a business situation, I will mention the name and location of my office and a bit about what I offer. If I am in a social situation, I might want to give an entirely different spin on my personal situation or interests. You are giving people enough information so that they can approach you and start a conversation easily, based on what you have told them.

Make your face available to your listeners. This helps them hear your speech. We need the clues on the face, especially in noisy conditions. Do not talk to the table. Keep your hands away from your face. Did I mention that you should swallow any food in your mouth before speaking? Do.

Speak to the people seated the farthest away from you. The greater the distance, the more effort will be required. *The more people, the slower you will need to speak, especially if it is noisy.* Some turning of the head will help more people get your message.

Do not rush your introduction. Get all the way up before you start speaking. Look around the room, own your space, and then address the group. Take your time. You don't want to be the person who acts like you aren't worth everyone's time (at the same time, don't take noticeably longer than other people). Observe how others do it and identify the models of clear identification.

Make a point of lingering after the meeting to allow people to make contact with you. That is the point of this whole exercise, isn't it? So slow down, be approachable and open to people, and chat with people who are around you. Now you are ready to get to know people and *really* introduce yourself.

The Intelligent Interview

Dale, in his mid-thirties, had an interview scheduled with a potential investor who could bring a lot of money to Dale's start-up in Silicon Valley. I made an appointment for a trial interview before Dale met with the financier. This investor could make all the difference in Dale's future, and Dale didn't want to blow the opportunity.

"Hi Carol!"

Dale walked into my office wearing jeans, tennis shoes, and a tee-shirt with a commercial logo, and, yes, he intended to dress this way for the interview. "Everybody" Dale deals with on a daily basis dresses this way, and he told me it did not occur to him to do otherwise for his upcoming interview.

Here are some excerpts from my interview with Dale:

> Dale: "I'm the CTO of a growing company and I'm like exposed to speaking events and like investors and like I'm awkward with chitchat. Oh I can talk technology; otherwise it just peters out... I self taught myself. ... I like to break the ice with, ya know, with a little sarcasm, ya know, just to engage them quickly...I need to link it up to businesslike lingo, ya know, different slangs to kinda like, ya know, I hear people talking and they can say—like idioms?—to create conversation. ... But I'm not as articulate as I need to be, ya know, ... And my voice, it doesn't have like punctuation."

Dale knew the name of the investor and that was all. As "geeky" as he was (his word), he had not used the computer to gain advance knowledge about his potential investor; he knew no history, had made no plan, and could tell me nothing about the investor's pattern or personal characteristics. We went to the computer and learned the following within a few minutes:

How the investor presented himself (like wearing a jacket and slacks).

Details of personal history. Dale was surprised at how many details were shared—colleges, hobbies, sports—that would support social conversation. We found a previous investment that suggested that Dale's area of interest might be a very good match.

Preparing for the "Last Three Feet"

The real crucial link in the ...exchange is the last three feet, which is bridged by personal contact, one person talking to another.

—*Edward R. Murrow*

I am looking at this information on the website for social information: to identify potential small talk and bonding topics, and cues for meaningful relationship and conversational development in "the last three feet" of the investor interview—the face-to-face interaction. Here is exactly where Dale (and his generation) is ill at ease. It seems that the greater the personal investment in technical wizardry, the less awareness of the subtleties of human communication. Because they have had so much success outside traditional hierarchies, they cannot recognize the complex social structure of the greater community or understand how to successfully negotiate their way to amicable and productive situations with people who do not come from their age group. Flexible communication skills come into play in all interactions and will make all the difference in the perception of your value. Dale's "value" would undoubtedly be on the line. What do you think was my first impression of him? ("Hi Carol!") The first words that come to mind are likely to be "rude, juvenile, and arrogant."

I have thought long and hard about Dale's behavior and have decided that he simply does not know better. And he does not know what he does not know. He needs schooling in dress and address, in courtesy and formalities, in social conversation and in strategy. I advised him to look into the work of Marty Nemko, the Bay Area Career expert, to learn more successful behavior. For his take on job interviewing, go to http://www.martynemko.com/articles/advanced-course-in-interviewing_id1432.

Some Communication Tips for Dale

1. Make the interview a two-way conversation.

Never show up for an important interview without knowing everything you can about your contact and their operation. You must go to their website and see how they position themselves, their reports and mission, what they have in the pipeline, and who the important players are. They have your résumé in front of them. You need to walk in with equal information about them. Your knowledge will become evident—don't force it—during the interview and will make a very good impression. *You are turning an interview into a conversation.* They'll know that you are smart, that you are a self-starter, and that you are ready to work.

The company is trying to solve a problem by hiring a solution. You can help them see you as a solution by probing in an empathic, nurturing manner to clarify the problem. "Can you tell me more about that? Is there a recent example? What solutions have you tried already? Why do you suppose they failed? What did that cost you? Have you given up?"

You can see this is a long way from sitting passively and just trying to answer their questions. You can be an equal partner in defining your suitability for their perceived problem. You will not only hit the ground running, but you'll be way ahead of everybody else. Dale had the technical smarts but not the communication smarts. He would have been caught flat-footed.

2. Consider how you speak.

You need to increase your awareness about your communication characteristics when under stress. Here are some places to start:

Preparation habits: You have probably heard that anticipating questions and preparing your answers in advance is a good thing. It is. But have you heard of "too much of a good thing"? You may be so over-prepared that your sentences are spoken in the flat, hurried manner of the memorized rather than the conversational and melodic style of the spontaneous answer. This also adds to your stress because you can now worry about not remembering your answer!

What to do: Never prepare complete sentences, but outline your pertinent information using numbers, words, and short phrases. You are now free to select the supporting language in a more natural way that is appropriate to the relationship you are currently in.

Point of view: Let's say that you are asked why you are interested in this job, and you respond along these lines: "Well, I've always loved working with people. Even when I was a little girl, I just wanted to help people. I guess I was just a little mother, hahaha. In high school I was a candy striper at the Catholic Hospital and—I think it was a Catholic hospital—but now I'm not sure. Anyway, it was so much fun getting to ..." They do not care. They are getting bored. You are rattling on from the point of view of your personal experience about which no one is the least bit interested.

What to do: Consider every question from their point of view. *Why are they asking?* and *What do they want?* should be questions you are asking yourself so you can get right to the point. Perhaps something like, "I've had twelve years in customer service positions, with four years managing the whole department. Your position clearly demands a strong service component in areas where I've had experience."

Speech clarity: You will be anxious to talk and may speak too rapidly for your listener. Since your information is old to you, it will not feel as if you are speaking rapidly. But consider their point of view (again). They are hearing this stuff for the first time and need to process your language to extract the meaning. Many people are so anxious to race through the *words* that they neglect the speech sounds necessary for projection to other people.

What to do:

- You will speak quite differently in a real communication exchange than when you are by yourself, so enlist a friend to interview you with prepared questions. Record this interview, wait for a while, and then listen to the recording. Nothing else will be more convincing or effective in inducing change. You will want to practice, consciously speaking in a more deliberate style; you did say you wanted to be more articulate, didn't you?

- You can become aware of the mannerisms and 'empty language" (ya know) that you DON'T know you use. You may be appalled, but at least you'll become aware – the first step for change.

- You will have done the work that will help you use this book more effectively to help you speak your best. You will be glad that you did this when you are in the actual interview.

I have heard of an individual who was hired just on the basis of his fluency and demeanor during the interview. He didn't fit the job description, but the interviewers were so impressed with his communication skills that they hired him anyway. They would invent the job that could best use his skills. I choose to believe this story; not only that, I think that it could happen again.

Leave Me Voice Mail, and Let Me Tell You How

I'll bet you like voice mail messages sent to you to be complete, clearly spoken, to the point, and lasting not one second longer than they have to. So do I, and so do most people I know. We can elevate the level of voice mail messaging with the following points. I will go over the beginning, the middle, and the end (how original!), and await your perfectly designed calls.

The Beginning

Identify yourself clearly. Even if they are friends or regular customers of yours, do not assume that they will know you immediately by your voice. It really is a discourtesy to make them guess your identity (which will distract them from the content of your message). State your name and connection with care. Be especially articulate if you have an unusual or foreign name. What is so familiar and easy for you to say may be a smear of unintelligible sounds to another, especially since they cannot see you. Speak your name as if it were written in boldface or underlined to get a more deliberate speaking style. Then pause ever so briefly before and after you say it to allow them to put it together.

Even if you are calling a friend, please understand that people know a number of Joans, Johns, and Pats. Add your last name and do not put their patience to the test.

Always say your complete phone number right after your name. You should not assume they know the area code. Here again, you must remember that your return phone number, so familiar to you, may be new information for your contact. Say your phone number with clarity and deliberation. Remember, people have hearing losses, rooms have noise, and lines have static. And if you leave just one number unintelligible, the whole effort is wasted. When that happens to me, I have a choice of dialing all ten possible guesses or just giving up. Guess which one I'm likely to choose!

The Message

When we make phone calls these days, we know better than to expect to actually get the person live on the line. It pays to think through a voice mail message before you pick up the phone. Since there is no one there to ask questions, you have to take the responsibility of organizing the necessary points of your message by imagining what your listener will need to know.

Do leave a message. Do not just say, "Call me." Say, "I want to have that lunch I promised you. Would Thursday or Friday next week work for you?" Or, "I'm calling to discuss a delicate personnel issue. I'll be at this number for the rest of the afternoon." Or, "I want to report a leak in the water cooler." By leaving a message, you're advancing the communication efficiently.

Get right to the point. I like it when the caller gets to the bottom line right at the beginning. ("Carol, we have to cancel our meeting. We'll need to reschedule for tomorrow. Could you call me right away? I'm at ...") Explanatory detail may be added at this point, but don't make me listen to a narrative, a winding path going heaven knows where. Drives me nuts.

Speak to just one topic at a time. We have only so much attention capacity. You are more likely to get a prompt response if your stimulus is efficient. Also, consider the possibility of your message being forwarded to or accessed by someone else. You may not want that additional topic to be broadcast. Voice mail is not a secure medium.

Indicate the urgency of a response or that you're expecting a return call, if appropriate. You can also indicate, "There's no need to call back, if ..."

The Closing

Again, repeat your name, phone number, and the best time to reach you. Make it easy for them to return your call. The repeat allows for an accuracy check of your phone number. Cell phones are frequently a less-than-perfect carrier of the voice, and the user must take special care to reduce the noise level around you and to repeat the phone number. Respecting the time of the person you have called is the first step in telephone courtesy. And courtesy is never a waste of time.

Getting Your Point Across

When a person wants to improve oral presentations, the first thing I think of is usually the last thing that person thinks of: the organization of the material. Controlling the sequencing of your ideas is the single most important act necessary to clear communication. The human brain does not want a flurry of words and images, but a thoughtfully structured stream of relevant and logical information. For example, business leaders especially want you to announce your topic immediately and make it clear why they should listen.

You may recall the discussion of the difference between self-expression and communication "Speaking Your Mind Effectively," so neatly summarized as "Get to the point." I cannot improve on that.

Jim was on the verge of losing his job in a financial organization because he could not get to the point of his presentation in a timely fashion. It was driving his boss and others crazy. It was not unusual for there to be a chorus of "Get to the point!" during his talks. How embarrassing! Jim had a habit of delivering his personal experience narrative: "... so I called the comptroller of that bank, but he was out so I had to talk with his secretary and she told me that the records would not be available, so would I call back later that day ..." Jim was shocked that all he needed to say was something like "The records will be available later this afternoon." Jim was a personable and chatty fellow so this statement seemed abrupt, incomplete, and rude to him. He was very good at schmoozing and social conversation, where self-expression was a plus. But he had to learn that the concerns of the business audience take precedence in the presentation of information. His personal experience was irrelevant to the communication.

Let's learn from Jim's experience and consider some ways of organizing materials that have the listeners in mind. You will recall that this is the very definition of "communication"—to make common. We will consider two possible formats that I have found to be extremely useful in organizing your thoughts and information. Jim tried out both of these approaches repeatedly so he could gain some confidence in using them and so he could choose the most appropriate for his current situation.

The best all-purpose formula for your remarks is one you've heard before:

> Tell'm what you're going to tell'm.
>
> Tell'm.
>
> Tell'm what you told'm.

This is also known as having a beginning, middle, and end, but that sounds so dull! Have an opening statement that tells people the general nature of your topic and why they should listen. This is the best place to catch their interest and where they will decide if they are going to pay attention. Since people tend to remember what is at the very beginning of a presentation—the principle of *primacy*—get to your point or conclusion right away:

> *You can expect a reshuffling of management.*
>
> *Company X has become competitive.*

This city needs new leadership, and I think we have the answer!

The SPCA deserves your continued support.

In these examples, your remarks may be a report or part of an ongoing operation, and people are just interested in an update. What if you have to engage a *new* audience in a topic with which they are not so familiar?

Use your opening statements to construct a bridge between your listeners and your topic in order to engage their interest. Not only can you tell'm *what* you are going to tell'm, you can show them *why* they will care. A really good way to do that is to talk about them and the benefit to them for listening to you. Take the time to get in touch with what people are thinking and wanting so you can address these issues early. If the audience feels heard and understood, or if they feel intrigued by your opening material, they are more likely to listen to you. Here are some examples of this principle in application at work:

Sales: A common error made by many earnest beginning salespeople is to cite the features of their product ("This knife sharpener is made of super-duper steel, tested in multiple laboratories, and is approved by the Good Housekeeping Institute") rather than the benefits to the buyer ("Think of all the dull and useless knives you have cluttering your kitchen drawer. Will you have to buy a whole new knife set, or would you rather have an easy way to sharpen them up into fighting trim?").

Research: "This new vocabulary test has been tested on 800,000 children in the Seattle area with multiple trial applications on minority populations ..." or "Like most teachers, you have been frustrated in providing your youngsters with language-appropriate literature because of insensitive vocabulary testing procedures." A teacher, in this example, is going to be more sensitive to the needs of the students than to the characteristics of the test.

Philanthropy: "The cost of an education for a deaf child starts at $35,000 for just basic school placement and not counting the needs for medical attention and hearing aids ..." or "I wonder what it's worth to you to be able to hear music, the voice of your mother, or your first child's cry." Now we are at the emotional heart of the issue when we cite the importance of hearing in forging human relationships.

Your point will make a bull's-eye if it is aimed at where people are actually listening, which is their concerns and emotions.

Tell'm ... and not just once, either. Be prepared to repeat the most important message several times in the course of your remarks. Because this core message is embedded in the larger language context, your listeners will not necessarily recognize your major points. By repeating the core message several times, slightly varied, the listeners are confident they have found the intended message. You are probably concerned that the audience will be offended by the repetition. Think of it as emphasis. I doubt that they will actually notice it consciously. But when someone asks them later what you said, they will most likely answer with your core message. In which case, you have made your point.

The "tell'm" part is called the body of your talk. This material needs to be organized in some way easy for the listeners to process or they will not be clear about your message. See if you can't organize your information under three subtopic headings. This format is simple but useful because it respects the cognitive capacity of the average audience and has saved many a speaker from floundering in a sea of confusing details. Look at your material to see if it lends itself to a three-part organization.

Announce this organization toward the beginning of your remarks. For example, "I am going to describe (1) the purpose of the study, (2) the testing procedures, and (3) the findings as they apply to three-year-olds." They now know what to expect, how to organize your remarks, and are more likely to get your point because they don't have to fight confusion.

Another example is, "I am sure you will want to stock the new Haviland Knife set because of its (1) superior construction, (2) handsome appearance, and (3) attractive pricing." You then offer this information organized in this systematic way.

Jeff knew he was to make his reports easier for the listeners to process but discovered that this format also made it a lot easier for him to think about his material and to exclude extraneous information.

Tell'm what you've told them. Closers are as important as openers since people tend to remember the ending material of a presentation (the law of *recency*). You end with a summary statement, some applications or ramifications of your information, or a review of the major points. You're giving them the chance to confirm their understanding and you are staying in control of your message.

This "tell'm" sequence—I call it the skeleton of the speech—provides the basic structure of remarks that may last five minutes or fifty minutes. If you are confident of your skeleton, you can expand or reduce as the needs of the audience demand. Jim's skeleton becomes a stable structure of organization for his thinking and his talk. He became very confident of this organizational structure.

The Speaker

An organizational pattern brings great relief to a speaker because the simple skeleton structure is easy to remember and yet flexible in application. As elementary as this approach may appear, it is surprisingly difficult for some people to use. It requires them to get out of their own habitual way of narrating information and into a systematic format constructed for the listeners' point of view. To do this, you must complete the thinking process before you begin your talking. You must identify your major from your minor ideas and determine the most logical order to present them to your listener. You have surely heard that you should think before you speak? This bit of thinking and effort will give you greater confidence and fluency in expressing yourself.

The aforementioned Jim was practically teary when he tried to impose a systematic structure on his remarks. He's not stupid; he has just never had to do this before. If organization of material does not come naturally to you, instruction, effort, and repetition will be required to learn how to think in a new way, but it can be done. In Jim's case, I would have him e-mail me every day with a skeleton organization of some topic involved in his work until it became second nature to him.

The Listeners

Clear organization and repetition helps them get your point because the audience is experiencing a number of distractions, internal and external, during any presentation.

Internal:	Something you say sets them off on some other line of thought.
	They are thinking about that phone call they need to return.
	They are texting. When's lunch?
External:	Noise interferes with the message.
	Something about the visual scene is preventing concentration.

More Challenging Circumstances

Tim was going to have to address the top leaders of his company (the "Big Dogs"), so we knew he had to have an even more sophisticated approach for giving information. What works with your average presentation does not work for the powerful people at the top who are likely to glance at their watches and who can interrupt you at will.

(In this regard, I would highly recommend the book, *Speaking Up* by Frederick Gilbert if you are in middle management and must make presentations to upper management. Gilbert knows what is necessary for effective speaking in the toughest of business situations based on direct interviews with individuals from both middle and upper management.)

Since his superiors liked getting to the bottom line as soon as possible, that's where Jim started. And he had no handouts and no slideware—just Tim and the bottom line. You'll have to imagine this bottom line as actually the tip of a pyramid, "bottom" meaning the final summarizing idea.

This single idea is actually a comprehensive statement that summarizes supporting information in a logically constructed pyramid. Let's say we lead with a statement, such as "We need to choose a new supplier of office paper." Big Dog may say, "So do it!" or he could ask, "What are our options?"

You now go down to a level of information that supports your bottom-line statement. You say, "That would be Taiwan or a company down in Milpitas."

The Big Dog can cut you off at any time, depending on how much time he wants to put into this. Let's say there are more questions. "What do we know about time and cost comparison?" But you foresaw this question and are ready to supply exactly this information for Taiwan and Milpitas. The pyramid of information looks like this:

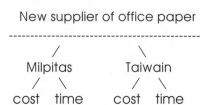

Notice how this simple idea of logical organization is entirely respectful of the listeners' need for clear sequence and of their time. It is completely listener-oriented. You are never giving them more information than they want nor any unrelated information.

But hold on! One of the older Big Dogs says, "Why are we spending our time talking about paper, for heaven's sake?" Like so many speakers, we've plowed right into an answer without clarifying the question. There is a narrative introductory structure that provides the necessary history of the issue. Use the following format: Situation, Complication, Question, Answer (SCQA) (see Minto in references).

> *Situation*: We have always bought all our paper supplies from Crown Company.
>
> *Complication*: They just had a huge fire and are going to close down.
>
> *Question*: Where are we going to get our paper?
>
> *Answer*: Here is where your information is appropriate. ("We need to choose a new supplier.")

With this format you are getting everybody nodding their heads in recognition and ready to receive your answer now that they know the relevance to the question in their minds. Note that the question is not at all obvious. There are a number of questions that could be asked. ("Should we send a condolence card?") The answer should contain only the information that bears upon the question in the logical order suggested.

Do this, and your particular Big Dogs will love it. Promise! But this thoughtful organization is harder to do than it sounds. You have a habitual way of organizing information (or not) that seems right to you, and this may be a stretch. Many people like to give information in the order that they personally experienced it. But who cares? Give people the information in the order that works best for them.

Look at some news stories in the paper and try to apply the SCQA and pyramid structure to the information. Many stories start with the complication. Figure out the statement that should precede it. Apply organizational logic. This makes for excellent reports, written or spoken. Make your Big Dog happy.

Smooth Small Talk

Do you admire those individuals who can go to a social or business function and chat freely with people, even strangers, with comfort and fluency? I would guess that you do, and I would also bet that you may be the person standing in the corner clutching a glass and feeling isolated. Or you are attached at the hip with the one person you know, watching others mingle, socialize, network and just enjoy each other.

At this point in your discomfort you probably are thinking: "Small talk throws me for a loop—I am ill at ease and feel stupid; *therefore* small talk is stupid, worthless, and to be avoided at all costs." I offer an alternative conclusion you should think instead: "Small talk is an extremely valuable communication skill, and I have not yet learned how to do it well." Let's take a closer look at this curious communication skill—so "easy" on the surface, so difficult in practice.

The Basics of Chatting

Small talk is a safe, warm verbal exchange between people that establishes friendly intent. It has the same function as an on-ramp to a freeway—a safe way to get up to speed for more meaningful conversation. We can also liken it to the volleying that precedes a real game of tennis, a warm-up period where you loosen up and take each other's measure. It is the most important communication skill you can develop because it is how you bring all new people into your life. From the board room to the bowling alley, human interchange has to start somewhere agreeable to both parties.

There is a lot to know about small talk because there is a lot happening between people during initial meetings. If you think that small talk is "idle chitchat" and just "talking about the weather," you have been fooled by the superficial characteristics of initial conversation. It is, in fact, the time to make nice murmurings to each other, to present a smiling face, and establish yourself as an agreeable person. You need to be willing to spend some time discussing some aspect of shared mutual reality—the game you both just saw, the crowded bus, or the weather. It wouldn't hurt to be thinking about suitable topics before you engage others. Look around. What catches your eye? (I am talking about American customs here; other cultures handle initial conversation differently.)

Your First Problem Is Your Self

Self-consciousness is frequently our first companion at a social event. I won't waste a paragraph telling you all the ways self-consciousness manifests itself; you can write that paragraph yourself. But there is an answer to this discomfort, and it's right in front of you—investing your attention in other people instead of yourself. (The same goes for public speaking, by the way.) Caring about others will also make you a more kindly, attentive conversational partner. As Dale Carnegie put it,

"You can make more friends in two months by becoming interested in other people than you can in two years by trying to get other people interested in you." Let's say you want to open a conversation with a stranger and are prepared to offer them your attention. STOP! You first must be sure that your interest is offered politely.

Politeness

I am not talking about particular behaviors here like "good manners"; politeness is the observance of appropriate warmth and respect.

Warmth: You want to exude a positive feeling, smiling, leaning forward, and extending your hand to these new people. You want them to know that you are happy to meet them. (Because they are probably a bit on edge, too.)

Respect: You are sensitive to their need for distance and formality and are careful not to violate their space and dignity. So you don't use their first name until they tell you to, you don't touch them (other than the handshake), and you don't make personal inquiries. Every culture I know observes hierarchical differences, and you need to find those out, especially if you are trying to do business with them. This information had apparently skipped over Dale (a few pages back), who was ignorant of the people part of negotiation.

Just last week I introduced two people to each other, both of whom I had known for a long time and liked equally. My pleasure in introducing my friends to each other turned into appalled horror as the fine line between warmth and respect was violated by my short, animated, lively friend who inadvertently invaded the physical space of my tall, perhaps more refined, friend. Ms. Refined finally told Ms. Lively to get out of her space and that she did not like her gestures so close to her face. Ms. Lively was crestfallen, baffled, and hurt. Ms. Refined was irritated and insulted. From my vantage point, I could see that it was a clear violation of personal space. There was nothing to be done but to mollify feelings separately. And I was so disappointed that these two fine people had such an uncomfortable experience. Even the best of people can make mistakes and suffer social embarrassment.

Don't Share Your Problems

Now what do I say? So you talk about the business convention, the music, the food, and—yes—the weather. You must learn to love the weather as a topic. It is a shared reality, neutral and safe. Not every topic is appropriate for social conversation, especially when meeting people for the first time. You avoid the unpleasantness of your recent release from jail, critical comments about others, and matters of politics, race, or religion. (There is much more on the development of conversation later. At this point, just know to Be Nice.)

(As for handling the unpleasantness of other people, please get your hands on Daniel Menaker's book, *A Good Talk*, p. 133. I cannot improve on his extensive and lively discussion.)

It really is a matter of context. Banter and debate in the frat house is one thing—and a very good thing, indeed. This is the time for engaging with new information and ideas, to form your opinions, and to test your ability to go toe-to-toe with new ideas. Heated exchanges at the bar mitzvah are quite another matter. In a community or social event, you show respect for the host by making sure that conversation remains civil. Here's a trick that works for me when dreadful differences appear: turn off my attitude and cultivate curiosity or interest in their point of view. Assume that the other person is intelligent and well meaning, that she came to her point of view for very good reasons (as far as she's concerned!), and that this presents a safe opportunity to learn something and perhaps change my perspective. Withhold judgment and try to understand. You just might learn something. I usually do.

If your attempts at small talk are anything but smooth, there are good reasons for that. Take your pick:

1. You don't even know that it is a particular branch of communication that has an important purpose and form, that it requires a certain amount of ritual and formalities that can be learned, and that these formalities differ among various cultures.

2. You may not have been taught the skills of conversation; you may not have even had a chance to observe them in action. The social life of your parents will play an important role here.

3. You have not valued social conversation as an important skill. You have so thoroughly convinced yourself that it is stupid, empty, and insincere that you feel it is beneath you.

4. The technological distraction. I am getting more and more requests for help in (Get this!) "off line chat"! Modern technology has provided so much material for attention (e.g., video games, social media) that used to be provided by direct contact with other people. Clients speak of whole childhoods spent at a computer monitor. While there is much to be gained from online information, it does not teach you social skills, effective listening, or reading other people, much less the verbal skills of conversation with others. Oh yes, it can tell you much about these topics, just like a book can tell you much about ballet; it doesn't mean that you can dance when you are done with the book.

But if you were born really lucky, your family sat down to dinner together every night and talked with each other. You heard the conversational interaction of other people, observed turn-taking and courtesies. Your parents entertained other people in your home, casually or formally, and you were expected to make an appearance, handle introductions, and learn to take care of the guests. When you called an adult "Bill" (because your parents did) your parents let you know that he was "Mr. Hanson" to you. You didn't stuff your mouth with cookies from the plate you were offering to guests; always the guests come first (I had a tough time learning that one myself). Are your hands clean? Is your hair combed? You've got to be carefully taught. And you will be so grateful that you were when the time comes for graceful social behavior in situations that matter to you.

Having a Purpose

Think about having a clear sense of purpose when you go to the social event. Purposes are like a destination or a "float plan," a motive force that guides you to seek out the people you want to meet, to get your business cards out there, to make new acquaintances, and to find a new job. You are not just bouncing around on random waves. You have a right to move purposefully, make choices accordingly, and manage your time. Without a sense of purpose, you are fair game for anybody who wants to monopolize your attention. In other circumstances, your purpose could as well be "to please my mother," "to meet my new neighbors," or "to enjoy the thrill of our victory." That's fine.

Have you noticed how much more at ease you are when you volunteer to help at some social gathering? Pouring wine, helping with coats, checking people in, and being part of the action make you belong in an important way. It gives you a purpose.

Social or Business?

Many social opportunities are strictly social, and even the presentation of a business card would be in bad taste. Weddings and funerals come to mind. You'll need to be observant and make this judgment. If mention of business feels awkward, it is probably best to try to make a date for later contact. There is discussion of business application at the end of this section.

Looking Closely at Conversation

Let's dissect the elements of human communication so we can slow it down a bit for those who would really appreciate the 'baby steps' of chat. We'll take a look at what you say, how you say it, and how you look when you say it.

What *Do* You Say?

Topics do not spring to your tongue with a perfect stranger. You have to invent a topic. I offer a three-step process to get a topic in play: Anchor, Reveal, Encourage (ARE).

Anchor the conversation with a topic that is part of your mutual shared reality. What do I mean? Something like this: "That is a gorgeous display of flowers on the stage," "They've certainly got a lot of booths set up," or "It looks like it's just pouring outside."

Note 1: *These are safe pleasantries that establish friendly intent and get the ball rolling.* Understand that neither of you is really interested in the weather or the flowers. You are making friendly noises at each other to see if you're available for connection or friendship. Don't waste time worrying about these "stupid" topics; they are simply safe ways of getting started to more interesting topics. Everybody understands this and will generally play along. Wanting to be original and clever is understandable but dangerous because you may end up paralyzed and self-conscious with your effort.

Would you be surprised that I am sometimes hired by young men to help them craft a sure-fire "line" to charm women? I send them to the internet where—you won't be surprised—they can find many sites dedicated to the pursuit of ladies.

Note 2: *If you are the one to start the conversation, you will be perceived as the leader, the adult.* You are taking the social risk, assuming the burden of coming up with topics, remembering names, introducing people, and moving the conversation. You are making other people comfortable and creating the rapport that leads to sociability and to business development. You can see there is a real payoff to showing initiative in small talk.

Of course the simplest starter is simply, "Hi, my name is ..." (Smile, make eye contact, and offer a handshake.) "It's nice to meet you! What's *your* name?" (Done! Now was that so hard?)

What you do now is crucial to the probability of having an interesting exchange. You will be meeting Carilyn a bit later; here's what she thought would be the way to proceed: "I just smile a lot and keep asking questions!" Carilyn was astonished that I did not heartily agree with her (but I was nice about it).

Reveal: Now go on to say something that has more information about *you* (using the Anchors mentioned above).

> "I wish I could get my gladiolas to be that large."
>
> "There weren't nearly as many people here last year."
>
> "Wouldn't you know I'm wearing my new shoes and my umbrella's in the car!"

What have we achieved here? We've supplied more information for the person to respond to, and we've made ourselves a bit vulnerable by giving away this free information.

And how does this make the other person feel? They will find you more likeable and will be more willing to trust you. It is difficult to trust those who reveal little because we can only guess what they're thinking, feeling, and believing. For trust to be mutual both people must be open. With new friends or co-workers, we build trust over time by revealing more and more along the way.

Encourage: After you have made a more personal comment, it is time to invite the other person to speak. Get the ball into their court with a question. Using the examples above, you might say:

> "I don't suppose the current weather permits much gardening around here, does it?"
>
> "Have you been to this convention many times before?"
>
> "How did you manage to get in and stay so dry?"

Never forget that the person having the most fun is usually the one doing the talking. Don't hog the conversation. Think of a tennis volley where the action consists of a back-and-forth of the ball. Both people have to be involved, so make sure that you get the ball in their court whenever possible.

How You Say It

Because of the noise level and distractions that prevail at mixers and conventions, you'll want to pay special attention to the clarity of your speaking and the preservation of your voice. There is more specific discussion about dealing with noise at the end of this section.

Keep your statements short and simple if you want your conversation to be easily understood. Do not embark on any long stories because you *will* be interrupted, the topic will quickly shift to something else, and you will feel frustrated and foolish with the point or punch line yet to be delivered. Subtleties and unusual vocabulary will be lost in the hubbub, whereas commonalties will have better luck. Wit takes a drubbing when you have to repeat the line three times. Don't open any topics that do not lend themselves to shouting. ("I said she's a pain in the butt! Oops. Sorry.")

Keep your speech lively on the face. People speech-read faces far more than they realize. We are experts at deciphering the minute twitches of muscle that shape a speech sound or an emotional expression. You will be doing people a great favor if you consciously articulate your speech with more energy in the face.

Repeat the sentence, "Put the front of the tongue in the front of the mouth," and focus your attention on the anterior part of your speech mechanism as you make these particular speech sounds. I want you to have increased awareness of movement in the face. Your speech will be easier to see and hear if you try to place your speaking in this area. (No, I promise that you will not look as funny as you feel.) This area is known as the mask. Hum, or say, "uh-hum." You will notice the sense of vibration at the very front of your face. The clearest articulation ensues when you energize the articulatory movements in this area, like lip and tongue-tip sounds. This will help your conversational partners not only hear you better, but they will be able to *see* your speech better (see the section "I Wanna Be Articulate!").

You will surely notice that women's voices carry a lot better than those of men in rooms filled with conversation and noise. Men, your voices fit right into the ambient room noise spectrum. It is important for you to place your speaking more in the front of the face and be sure to add as much vocal variety as possible. The ear follows the musical voice. (See "Expressing Vocal Variety.")

How You Look When You Say It

People have a whole room full of other people they could approach in social gatherings. They look around and make a choice. You want them to choose you. So much easier than you approaching others, don't you think? All they have to guide their choice is the way you look. You have to figure out how to make yourself attractive. Read the sections in Chapter 5, specifically "Unifying Your Verbal and Nonverbal Messages" and "Becoming Approachable."

The next time you are in a room full of strangers, look around and ask yourself which people you would feel comfortable walking up to and starting a conversation. Who is attracting your favorable attention? Who would you avoid? And why? Figure out for yourself what you find attractive or scary and see if that information could be useful for you.

How you look is really important in social situations. Remember that people are reading you from a distance, and they're considering your wardrobe, grooming, and carriage in a glance. Obviously, you should try to look your best because people tend to believe that the better looking you are the more positive traits you have. Good-looking people are thought to be smarter, more successful, and just better in every way. Like it or not, this is just how it works. Of course, what is considered "good looking" varies with different cultures, but the generality still holds. Doing your best will be good enough; the effort will be perceived and appreciated.

Question: *But what do I wear?* Answer: If you are unsure, ask the host. Other people do. You'll feel more comfortable. For women especially, you need to develop the habit of wearing something eye-catching and interesting in your accessories (handbags, belts, scarves, pins, etc.). They provide a ready topic of conversation for the person who wants to get to know you. That fun or funny tee-shirt you have may be just the thing at a picnic or other casual events. The logo or artwork can lend themselves to easy conversation openers:

> "So you went to Northwestern, too?! When were you there?"
>
> "Do you like Betty Boop? I thought I was the only one!"
>
> "You must be an animal lover, too. Did you get that in Africa or here?"

There is much more material on wardrobe choices in "Business," later in this section.

Free Information

The most valuable tool you have for conversational development is the use of additional comments and facts beyond the opening anchor that allows the conversation to develop or go somewhere else altogether. If you don't do this, you will be stuck discussing the weather for how long? Way too long.

For example, you're on the way down the hall with the person who will interview you for a possible job. Here's the conference room with the impressive table and the sweeping view of the city. You say, "Great view!" He may fire back with a snappy, "Yeah." Now what? You need to add some further observations or information to keep the conversation flowing. You happen to see a striking glass high-rise out the window of the interview room. So you make one of the following comments:

> "That building is fabulous. It really looks great in morning light. I like the effect of the fog with the reflections coming off the building."
>
> "I hear the locals call that building 'the jukebox.' I can see why. We don't have anything like that at home in Seattle. We're still very proud of our Space Needle. Have you seen it?"

In these examples, you have taken the initiative to introduce some new personal comments that invite response. If
this person is at all sociable, he will recognize the friendly
intent and will respond to your effort. Let's say the person
responds to your overture in the following way: "No, to tell
you the truth, I've never noticed that effect with the fog. It
does look kinda neat. I'm usually too occupied to look out
the window!"

She may say nothing or follow up with, "Gosh, it's been
years since I've been to Seattle. The Needle—is still standing?
I saw it the first year it went up, for the World's Fair, I believe.
I was visiting my brother who works for Boeing. We made a
big family outing of it." This is the kind of response you want.
The person is going beyond the first topic to offer other possible topics (brother, Boeing, World's Fair), and you can now
go on to respond to any one of these possible topics. You need
to become as forthcoming yourself to make it easy for other
people to talk with you.

With this abundance of free information, conversational
exchange will be made much easier. You're giving the other
person more things to talk about; it's that simple. You need
to be patient to explore different topics, and for heaven's sake,
don't get struck dumb just because your first attempt falls flat.
When it's in your best interest to get the conversation flowing,
you need to be tough about persevering.

Pay attention to your own tendency to give minimal responses. These one-syllable responses—*yeah, no, uh-huh*—
are the greatest conversation killers out there. Make a pledge
to not allow yourself to offer such minimal responses. While it
is not quite rude, it definitely does not promote conversation.

When conversations sag and die, it will most likely be because of minimal responses and no free information. Take a
look at "Offering a Gracious Response" for more examples of
ways to encourage conversation.

Think about Business Bridges

Small talk can be developed into effective business social conversation. It is part of the communication skill set you need for the modern work world because you need to interview for positions, you need to meet new business contacts, and you need to expand your network of friends and associates.

Although business social situations expressly support business interchange, you need to observe the rituals and courtesies of regular social interchange. We know that people do business with people they know, like, and trust, *and* all things being equal, people will buy from a friend. Even when things are not quite so equal, I am more likely to buy from a friend. Aren't you?

You can turn the social interaction into effective business social conversation if you make a bridge from initial pleasantries to the business topic. You'll start with a neutral and pleasant observation to engage the individual and then develop the conversation according to your purpose:

> from pleasantries (e.g., "Isn't this a lovely event? What a gorgeous room!")

> to connection ("I just returned from India, but I'm sorry to say I didn't get a chance to visit your part of the country.")

> to business ("I'm hoping to make a connection with an Indian company that wants speech improvement for the call center personnel.")

Business get-togethers usually involve your meeting strangers as an individual and as a representative of your company. You are Patti Jones (an individual), and you are Patricia Jones (sales manager of a real estate company). There needs to be a professional component in your appearance that gives you visual credibility as a professional.

Take a look at the chapter, "Unifying Your Verbal and Nonverbal Messages." This information is especially important in business social situations when you will be observed and evaluated by many people who are deciding if you are the person they want to talk to.

Every industry has its own dress code, and you would do well to respect this code. It is extremely powerful in communicating that you belong to a group and know how to conduct yourself. It will be instructive (and entertaining) to compare the wardrobe concerns of two of my clients.

Subash works in the high-tech industry in Silicon Valley. He meets with people from the computer software industries and online media companies. Casual dress is the norm: khakis and open-collared shirts. In companies of approximately three hundred employees you will not see a suit or a tie. The C-level executives may wear a jacket. Some say you don't wear a tie until the company goes public.

Now take a look at Kate's world. She is a fashion stylist in San Francisco. Over dinner, Kate had told me that she had had an exhausting day yesterday.

She met with an executive from a large department store to discuss fashion seminars. For this appointment Kate needed a sleek, sophisticated, Audrey Hepburn look.

After that, she went home and changed for a meeting at an urban chic retail jean store—very "glam-rock," she told me. She went "boho," casual with elements of style—an interesting scarf and bracelets.

Then Kate met with a producer at Comcast to be considered as a host. For this she changed to casual, fun, funky stuff.

Finally she appeared on a panel on recent runway styles with Fashion Group International. (What *did* you wear, Kate? An Armani jacket over a shift dress, tights, and black stilettos with studs on the platform.)

She knows that her credibility is established with the first glance at her appearance. This is not the exclusive domain of female style mavens. Take a look at former mayor of San Francisco Willie Brown's book, *Basic Brown*, where he devotes a whole chapter on the details of his impressive wardrobe. He would think nothing of changing into four different outfits during the day to suit the demands of his appearances.

Most of us operate somewhere between the world of Subash, Kate, and Willie Brown. But we all need the awareness that wardrobe choices announce our knowledge and acceptance of the culture and define our role in it.

Making an Exit

"I was with this woman who just wouldn't stop talking about her terrible neighbors. I was just trying to think how to get away but every strategy seemed so rude!" Carilyn was a very nice lady. Too nice. Her very niceness made her a victim of social paralysis.

She was a lot better at getting into a conversation than getting out of it. That's because starting social contact is comprised of positive approach behaviors: smiling and nodding, eye contact, handshakes, and name exchanges—all very pleasant and affirming. Everybody is making nice. Carilyn is the queen of nice.

Then she would run out of superficial pleasantries, the topic had dried up, there appeared to be no conversational future, and she really wanted to move on, but how? Exit behaviors can be darn close to rejection; all those positive approach behaviors have to be reversed. Ouch! Carilyn felt that it was rude to purposely terminate a conversation because it would hurt someone's feelings. If *you* feel this way, you will get stuck in the unproductive situation that Carilyn has often suffered. You will be unhappy, resentful, and aware of the potential contacts walking around the room that are now out of your reach. As Dr. Phil would say, "How's that workin' for you?"

One of the most important uses of having a purpose in social situations is that it gives you a reason to disengage. The importance of your purpose must outweigh your desire to be nice. Just the simple exercise described here about killed Carilyn.

The first step: Make some remark (verbal or nonverbal) that notes the passage of time: "Looks like the food is about gone." "It's starting to get dark out there." "I need to find my friend who's waiting for me." As a last resort, just glance at your watch. This works because you are giving a cue to your partner that now is the time of leave-taking and giving them the opportunity to safely initiate the exit themselves. Most likely, they will want to "save face" and will be quick to respond with leave-taking.

The second step: There are people who will require more explicit leave-taking statements:

> "I've enjoyed talking with you. I really must move along now."

> "Perhaps we can talk some other time. I need to hook up with my partner."

> "I need to talk with some other people. I'm glad we had this time together."

> "I'm sorry, I've got to talk to that person over there, but I'm glad I've had the chance to get to know you."

> "It was good talking to you, but I need to go out and chat with a few more people. Perhaps we can meet some other time."

What you see here is a plausible excuse and a verbal bouquet. It really doesn't have to be much. It doesn't even have to be true. We're talking face-saving here.

The final step: If there is any more difficulty making your point, put out your hand for a handshake, say the person's name while making direct eye contact, and repeat the statement mentioned previously. Start to back away immediately.

Noise and Your Voice

I am frequently asked about the problem of losing your voice at a noisy party or convention. It is the perfect storm of lousy communication conditions. People find themselves screaming in the evening and being without a voice the following morning. This is very bad for teachers or speakers who must use their voice for their work.

People are hardwired to talk louder than the ambient noise level. The louder the surrounding sound, the louder you have to talk to be heard. You've noticed that you automatically speak in hushed tones in very quiet places, haven't you? This is an unconscious attempt to establish an appropriate signal-to-noise ratio. You are doing the same (but opposite) adjustment when you find yourself yelling at a party, but here you pay a painful price for the extreme effort: vocal fatigue and strain and laryngitis. So the obvious first thing that you can do is to reduce the noise whenever possible.

Sometimes it only takes a request to get the volume from the sound system lowered. If nobody says anything, it will be assumed that it is okay. So say something.

Move Away from the Noise

It always amazes me how people are willing to tolerate the discomfort of room noise when they could reduce the assault by taking just a few steps away from the noise source. You can position yourself behind some kind of barrier to the loudspeaker, or you can lead your conversational partner around a corner. It also helps a little if you turn away from the noise source. You notice our ears are built to be maximally functional for sounds that we face. So turn your back to the noise. And it really helps catch your partner's speech if you are willing to cup your hand behind your ear when he is speaking. It's surprising how well this technique amplifies someone's speech.

Get closer to your conversational partner. In extremely loud conditions you may have to get your face within inches of the other person's face in order to understand what he is saying and to make yourself heard. Many people keep a distance and speak with their usual articulation level. Worse, you keep this "closed mouth" form of speech at the same time that you are forcing your voice to be heard. You will have added physical discomfort to your psychological unease. And people will still have trouble understanding what you just said.

Drink water! Actually, the time to load up on water is several hours before the vocal strain begins. I'll spare you the juicy physiology, but trust me, it makes your vocal folds much more comfortable and capable of staying that way through several hours of demanding conditions. The hard stuff (alcohol) is just that—hard on your vocal folds. Let me note that the likelihood of saying smart, appropriate comments intelligibly is not directly related to your alcoholic intake, even though it feels that way. You will not be nearly as witty as you think. But you may be loud—very loud indeed.

Keep it light. In noisy circumstances, it's a good idea to try to save the long, meaningful conversations for a more comfortable time.

The Last Word about Small Talk

It is the nature of small talk to be light on its feet and change direction willy-nilly. You think you are developing the topic of how bad the traffic is getting to the party, but somebody offers the comment about the Doyle Drive construction, which prompts someone else to mention, yes, they saw that when they were on the way to the Walt Disney museum, which by the way, is really good.

This is the fun of small talk: you never know where you'll end up. I liken it to the flow of jazz when players riff off each other and improvise.

This will be disconcerting to some who would like a steadier and more predictable topic treatment; folks with hearing problems are among this group. They will have just thought of their observations on traffic problems when the group has swung over to the George Lucas development close to the Disney museum. You cannot stem the tide, discipline the jazz, or regulate the flow of good small talk. Let go. All you can do is relax and appreciate what the players bring to the social song and offer your chirp now and then.

As a matter of fact, we have been occupied with conversation on the most functional, instrumental, and remedial of levels with special attention to business applications. Some would say that real conversation begins only after business needs have been met, and you talk for the sheer pleasure of it. To salute that capacity, I want to quote from a description of the conversational style of the French Enlightenment philosopher Denis Diderot just to acknowledge the heights that may still be possible in this verbal realm of ours. Diderot's conversation was

> enlivened by absolute sincerity, subtle without
> obscurity, varied in its forms, dazzling in its flights
> of imagination, fertile in ideas and in its capacity to
> inspire ideas in others. One let oneself drift along
> with it for hours at a time, as if one were gliding
> down a fresh and limpid river, whose banks were
> adorned with rich estates and beautiful houses.
> (*The Economist*)

One can only imagine. And wish.

For more basic information about social conversation, I would suggest that you listen to my audiotapes and CD called *The Serious Business of Small Talk*. Go to Conversationmatters .com and get on the mailing list. Read some of the excellent books available; see my citations page in the back. I give special recommendation to the book *A Good Talk* by Menaker for a most enjoyable survey of interesting observations beyond the purview of pedestrian self-help books.

Speaking in Front of People

Public speaking does represent the big leagues of human communication—big in the sense of opportunities to demonstrate leadership, influence people, and build your own future. Also, big in dread for many people. This sets up a defeatist cycle because the anxiety can prevent people from developing the skill set that once learned, would prevent the anxiety in the first place. Information and coaching can break this cycle— I've seen it work hundreds of times—and I promise that you can turn *terrified* into *terrific*. I will tell you about Mary H., a ministerial intern at my church as she finished her academic training for the ministry. After her first appearance in the pulpit, members of the congregation came to me. "Carol, you have to do something with that child's voice. I could not understand a word she said!" Other such comments suggested that the ministry was a poor choice for her. I routinely volunteered my services as a speech coach for all the interns, and the ministerial relations committee suggested to Mary that she work with me. She dutifully appeared in my office.

On a scale of one to ten, Mary started pretty much at a two, and that two was due solely to the quality of her content. Eyes down, practically whispering, she rapidly read through her sermon as if she were getting punished. I worked with Mary in a straightforward manner and was, frankly, impressed with how responsive she was to my suggestions. She left my office at a level five, I would say, and I felt pretty good about our work together. Come Sunday, and she went up to the pulpit with her sermon and scored a perfect ten. I simply could not believe what she had done with her training between the time that I had seen her and her appearance on the pulpit.

Success is usually much more gradual. It turned out that Mary was naturally gifted but didn't know it. And she had never had any speech training whatsoever. Moreover, she was able to incorporate the new power into her self-image. When she heard what she *could* do (in my office, on my tape and video recorders) she was determined that was what she *would* do. The more she believed in herself and her capabilities, the more she let her light shine.

She was clearly a new person and the congregation was quick to tell Mary how well she had done. I got a lot of thumbs-up from those who knew I had worked with her. I saw Mary several more times during her term, and she continued to amaze me with her aptitude and responsiveness. And—wouldn't you know it?—she was chosen to give the graduation speech at her commencement. Yes, I helped her with it and, yes, once again she performed way beyond anything I had given her.

So here were all these people applauding Mary after her triumphant commencement address, and here was this speech coach in the back of the hall, sobbing.

So, readers, I'll tell you everything I told Mary, just as I told Sandie when she was informed by her boss that he expected her to be the master of ceremonies at an upcoming regional sales conference.

Sandie, an otherwise competent and confident young woman, started sweating the minute her boss casually mentioned her appointment. She knew that this was an opportunity for personal advancement, and she was both flattered and astonished that her boss thought she was capable of this important role. Like many people, she had had some previous unpleasant experiences in public speaking that left a bad memory.

She was afraid of failure, rejection, and looking stupid. The more she envisioned these negative outcomes, the more she flooded her head with anxiety and paralysis; she put herself in the worst possible situation to deal with her challenge. Even Sandie knew she was bringing this on herself. All you have to do is decide that something is fearsome and that you are incapable, and your body responds with adrenaline to help you deal with this emergency. The heart pounds, the hands and knees shake, the breathing gets strange, and you start to sweat. My, how unpleasant it is! Put an image of disaster in your head, and the body tends to think that it is real. Sandie could not begin to prepare her remarks until her attitude turned around to a more positive direction. In her case, and perhaps in yours, dealing with stage fright is the first issue.

Sandra had been told that she would feel more comfortable picturing the audience in their underwear. Apparently this is supposed to make you feel superior to your audience so you won't be afraid of them. Have you heard that one, too? Who thinks up such nonsense?

Look at your audience as people who really need something that you are privileged to give them. The real key to comfort is exactly opposite of this underwear arrogance; it's an attitude of *service*. I had Sandra think of how she felt and behaved when she entertained guests in her home. She would be focused on their comfort and enjoyment, wouldn't she? Think of your audience as guests. The more she planned with this in mind, the happier she became because she stopped thinking about herself and spent her energy designing a program that would delight her audience and her boss.

Your problem is your own egocentricity. Consider this inner language: *What will they think of me? Will they criticize me? Everyone will be looking at me!* What's the common thread here? Me! That's egocentricity. Realize how adolescent such self-centered preoccupation is. It was normal then; it's inappropriate now. Going from self-centered to other-centered is the way out of this discomfort. Take a look at the section preceding this one, "Speaking Your Mind Effectively." Focusing on your listener/audience first helps you choose more effective language *and* removes the preoccupation with yourself. You probably greatly overestimate people's interest in you in the first place. They are mostly involved in their own agenda and fantasies. Think about how you are in an audience. Many times you fake attention to a speaker as you plan your vacation in your head. Sandra saw that she was actually competing with people's preoccupations rather than their criticisms. This idea alone helped Sandra shake off a lot of her apprehension. She realized that the group *needed* her energy and focus to guide them to information of real value to them.

The speaker can help the audience by engaging their motivation and curiosity. I like the image of the audience as a cold stove. This stove is just sitting there, cold and inert, until you provide the fuel and light the fire. What is in their self-interest is good kindling. Then light it with your passion. This warms everybody, including you. This is actually your job as a speaker. You would like to just start with a nice warm, receptive audience, but you are more likely to start with a cold stove—so get busy and deal with the situation. Speaking to their self-interest (kindling) ignited by your enthusiasm (fire), you'll start the action yourself. This is great fun!

As Sandra focused on the needs of her audience, she came up with imaginative ideas for themes and listener entertainment. Much to her astonishment, she was actually looking forward to the conference and relishing the fun she was going to have. I asked her to call me right after the conference to tell me how it went, and I got the most wonderful message I could want: "Dr. Fleming! I was a star!" Warning: being a star is highly addictive.

One way of keeping you genuine and comfortable with your audience is to arrive at the event early so you can meet and mingle with some of the audience and get in touch with what they are thinking and feeling. This will also serve to remind you that the audience is made up of ordinary people and that you are perfectly capable of talking to them. You will take this sense of relationship and comfort right up to the podium. You might even look for your new friends in the audience. This will make a huge difference in your tone of voice as well as your personal comfort.

Make Friends with Your Audience

Jason was a landscape architect hired by a developer to design a resort for the forested Tahoe area. Local residents in their cozy cabins on pristine, wooded acreage were up in arms over the proposal. They were NIMBY's (*Not In My Back Yard!*) A presentation to these residents about the resort had been planned for some time. At the last minute, the developer decided that he did not want to face the enraged locals and directed the architect to go up and do the community presentation.

Think for a bit how Jason—music-loving, garden-tending Jason—feels about (1) public speaking and (2) facing a hostile mob. Just like you would feel, I bet. As he put it, "I'd rather take a whuppin." I had Jason use this technique of arriving a day ahead of schedule and getting to know some people in the community. He was to make himself available for conversation in the local pubs, laundromats, and paths. He hung out at the library and talked to people about the project and made notes about *who* specifically was worried about exactly *what*. John Watts did not want his view of the forested skyline altered. Mary Cooksy wanted to continue riding her horses on the path that wound through the developed area. Others voiced concerns about pollution, traffic, and increased tourism. Jason took note of it all. We used this material to shape his opening remarks that went something like this:

I have heard that many of you have some serious questions about the resort development, and I don't blame you. This place is gorgeous just as it is. We will all feel more comfortable if I deal with some of these issues of concern right away.

Let me address the skyline issue. Many of you have homes in the same area that John Watts lives and do not want to lose that beautiful forest view by roofs and chimneys. You won't. Looking at this model, you will be able to see that the development is strictly within the valley here and will not impinge upon any of the vegetation visible to you.

And so on. Arriving early and meeting your audience helps you turn a presentation into a conversation, by allowing you to acknowledge their point of view immediately and, in this case, to disarm hostility.

Take advantage of public speaking opportunities on a small scale, at your church or community organization, to get some experience where performance skill is not crucial. Toastmasters International is great because it is widely available and supportive of speakers at all levels (Toastmasters .org). There are many chapters, and one is sure to fit your schedule. Make getting up and speaking a normal part of your life. Then the important speaking opportunities do not loom so large.

Leave as Little to Chance as Possible

This is the preparation credo of the professional speaker. Here is what that might look like for you.

Think about the goals of your presentation. Exactly what are you trying to achieve here? The clearer you are about that, the more likely your audience will get it. You can have several goals, of course: to explain a transaction, to solve a problem or present research, to impress your boss, to be clearly understood, etc. These goals give you a way to examine your efforts, take control of your presentation, and ensure that you are successful in achieving what you want with this presentation.

Think about your message. Can you succinctly state your *core message*? Let's say you have ten seconds on the elevator to let someone know your main point: can you do it? This is devilishly hard for the beginning speaker, but so helpful in your becoming clear yourself about your topic. This concise formulation may be the hardest part of your speech preparation.

It was hard for Mary to summarize her sermon in one meaty statement, but that's exactly where we would start our work each session. "Mary, what do you want the congregation to say when people ask them, "What did Mary talk about?" Not only does she need to articulate it clearly for herself, she needs to repeat it several times during her sermon for the congregation to get it

Consider the needs of the audience. Read "Speaking Your Mind Effectively" to remind yourself of the need to know your audiences as well as you know your material. And you need to know your material very well indeed because you must have your face lifted up so people can see, hear, and understand your speech better. You will be glad that you know your material well when it turns out that you have ten minutes instead of the forty-five minutes you prepared for. Or, you can't get your PowerPoint to work, and you have to wing it without A-V support. This is exactly what happened just this week to one of my clients who was speaking for the Rotary Club. The computer let him down, but he discovered—for the first time— that he was perfectly able to speak well without support. Isn't this wonderful thing to have happen?

You must have a considerably slower rate of speech when speaking in public than during typical conversation, given the acoustics of large rooms, the ambient noise, and the ubiquity of hearing loss. Take a look at "Fast Talkers" if you tend to talk fast.

Familiarize yourself with the setting. Is there a microphone? Lapel or standard? Is there a light on the lectern? If you need to walk around, you'll want to know if there are cords you need to be aware of and how people are seated. The more familiar you are, the more comfortable you will be.

Practice with family or friends. People who are really good get that way because they are willing to practice their presentations in front of others and take advice. You can, too.

One of your first goals is to be able to deliver your material without *reading*. Your goal is to be able to talk naturally to people while looking straight at them. You may want to use some notes to keep you comfortable and on course. I advise using three-by-five cards, with just a few ideas on each card, written in large print:

LIKE THIS

Now you can just glance at your cues to get your prompt without putting your head down and staring at the paper. If you do use a typed sheet, a font size at around 20 should be comfortable.

Rehearse with your audiovisual aids. You've been in audiences where the PowerPoint presentation or the slides became a major impediment to the talk and ate up huge amounts of time. This frustrates everybody, especially you, the speaker. You try to move your computer for better focus of the slide, you end up pulling out the electrical plug, you have to start all over, and on and on. We in the audience are not amused, and neither are you. This is a source of disaster that you can do something about by becoming smooth with the operation of your equipment. If you use slideware, be sure to read "You Plus PowerPoint."

This material above is a minimum! Do whatever you have to do to get all your ducks in a row because, at the time of the presentation, one of those ducks will go nuts! If everything else is under control, it won't be a big deal. That's the point of preparation.

Now that we have the equipment out of the way, what about you and your audience? Your audience should influence how you use your eyes, your voice, your word choices, and the organization of your remarks.

Eye Contact

Looking out at the people you're talking to is of critical importance. Your voice goes where your eyes go. Directing your voice out to people in the back of a room is easier if you are looking out that way. Look at "Soft Talkers" for more tips on getting your voice out there.

People will feel more connected with you when you make eye contact. You will have created more of a conversational relationship. When you are seeking out eye contact during a presentation, your audience will perceive you as authoritative and in control. People will feel that they should be paying attention to you and will. How much respect do you give a speaker who just holds her head down and reads the speech?

You can also practice projecting your voice to the back of the room by using this eye contact activity. Have some pals sit in the back row as part of your rehearsal. Their job is to let you know if you have made eye contact with them. Ask them each to hold up one hand with all fingers extended. They are to pull down a finger for every second of eye contact that they feel you have made with them. One finger should equal about one phrase of speaking.

You will be amazed at how effective this will be in teaching you how to make effective eye contact. The more amazed you are, the more you need to do this exercise until fingers are routinely folded down. Notice if the fingers in one part of the room are behaving differently than others. Here's your feedback that you are ignoring that section of the room.

Of course, you can also look into the eyes of other people not in the back. If you are feeling a bit uncertain, seek out the friendly faces, people who tend to nod encouragingly.

Content

In general, I would say that the most effective speeches are simple, straightforward, honest, and immediate. Just as people tend to talk way too fast, they also try to say way too much. Impact is diluted. I sometimes say, "Treat your speech as if your words were gold coins, not cheap popcorn." Your audience will take their cue from your deliberate, thoughtful sentences and accord you with attention.

Organization

Any presentation has to have a shape, a sequence of material that is easy to follow. Do *not* sit down in front of a keyboard and try to write your first sentence. But *do* imagine a flowchart of information. If you look at "Getting Your Point Across" and "Speaking Your Mind Effectively," you will find some guidelines on how to manage the flow of information for maximum clarity. These sections ask you to be mindful of your listeners' needs and capacities during the very act of formulating your speaking. Sometimes we overestimate the audience's ability to identify our main points and only mention these little jewels of meaning once. If you really want them to get it, then repeat it. Find ways to restate the meaning. Go ahead and tell them, "This is the most important point I want you to remember." Be sure and have this point repeated in your summation or conclusion so there is no doubt what was on your mind.

We also overestimate our listeners' ability to attend to our wonderful presentation. We can rattle on for an hour, but the attention of the audience is going to fatigue after about six minutes. So do something different! If you are planning a thirty-minute talk, for example, look for natural breaks in the material that allow you to introduce some variety. You could

- turn off the PowerPoint and just talk
- have a brief Q&A on a topic
- allow silence while the audience reads some material
- step out in front of the podium and chat
- play an audiotape or video
- have someone else read some material or discuss a point

Don't be afraid to be inventive and fresh. Just because you've always seen your predecessors drone on without variation doesn't mean that you can't do something new. Your audience will be grateful.

Projection

No, not the slides, your voice. Projection starts with upright posture. Your speech and voice come from a physical structure, your body, which must be positioned optimally for the projection of your talk. It is optimal to stand upright with your upper chest elevated, face your listeners, put your arms at your sides, ready for gesture, and position your feet slightly spread with your weight forward, allowing you to move easily in any direction.

I could put this in the negative and tell you not to slouch, lean over the podium, look down at notes, or fidget with a pencil or cord. In any event, you want your breathing to be unencumbered by poor posture because you are going to need good breath support to get your voice out there.

Projection is *not* just a matter of shouting or making your voice loud enough for people in the back to hear you.

It is a function of your *intent*, your *eyes*, and your *energy*. Let me explain.

You must *want* to fill a room with your presence. There's an attitudinal element here. Think of the roar of the lion filling the veldt. If you can hear him, you are on his turf. His voice defines his range of power. So you need to assume the voice of a leader whenever you speak. Because, as the speaker, you *are* the leader, even if the boss is sitting right in front of you. If you hold forth with a wimpy voice, you are defining your territory of dominance as very small indeed. You may not even sound like you are enthused about your topic or care about your audience.

Do you experience any of the following situations? It may be that you are naturally a soft-spoken individual, uncomfortable with raising your voice beyond a conversational level. There are some cultures that do not tolerate a strong voice, especially for females. You may have a cold or a very sore throat that makes speaking painful. You either need to use an excellent microphone and amplification to get your voice heard, or you need to let your voice announce your dominance of the room. Just don't make your audience strain to hear you. If you do, most of them will tune you out; they will have many other options to engage their attention.

Your voice will go where your eyes go. This is why it is such a bad idea to read your remarks. Your voice will be going right down on to your paper and not out into the room (unless you have a fancy glass prompter screen that allows you to read with your face up). You cannot speak to people directly unless you look directly at them. Even if there are three hundred of "them," you can seek out eyes during your talk. The listeners will see that you are looking at them.

Projection will cost you increased energy. If the room is not too big, I love to illustrate this principle with Koosh balls, those soft balls with rubber spikes of bright color. I start throwing the Koosh balls out into the (class) audience; they are to toss them right back to me. Soon the air is filled with flying Koosh balls, some of which I can catch and return. There is a point here. The closer you are to the stage, the softer the toss will be; the farther, the harder it must be thrown. This illustrates the added energy that is needed for projection out into the room.

The energy you need while speaking is associated with breathing capacity and control, voice production, and articulation. Please see "Soft Talkers" for the information you need here.

Speech Clarity

Public situations are usually noisy situations. Some of this noise will make it difficult for you to hear yourself since you are separated from the audience. You've been in audiences. Remember the lady unwrapping her candy s-l-o-w-l-y and the guy in the ripstop nylon jacket (they're noisy!). They and the paper shuffling, sniffling, coughing, chatting people generate noise that interferes with clear hearing. As a speaker you need to assume that noise is present.

Then there's the noise you *can* hear: traffic, air conditioning, restaurant clatter, etc. You need to deal with these by supplying clearly spoken language, where articulation cues are redundant. Please see "I Wanna Be Articulate!" for ways of increasing speaking clarity.

As far as language (actual word choice) is concerned, you must be guided by the general knowledge and vocabulary of your audience. You must speak to "where" they are listening. If you are a youngish person who would dearly love to impress your audience with your fancy new concepts and vocabulary, *it doesn't work*. When in doubt, simplify. You can apply this rule to just about everything in human communication.

Another sign of the beginner is the rushed speech. Rapid speech is really hard to follow in a public speaking situation.

Never forget that what is "old" to you is brand-new to your audience; allow them the time, in the form of pauses and slower rate, to process what you have to say. The more people listening, the slower you have to talk. Besides the other issues I have mentioned, the room acoustics and reverberations can cause problems with hearing a clear message. Cultivating a deliberate speaking rate will add greatly to your credibility and gravitas. Remember to treat your speech as if your words were gold pieces. Sound like you're somebody and you will be.

So, dear readers, I have told you everything that I told Mary, the ministerial intern. Now, you go out and make me proud of you!

You Plus PowerPoint

As I left the history lecture, I found myself saying, "That was the best PowerPoint presentation I have ever seen!"

I mulled over some of my memories of the history lecture.

Dr. David Bisno moved around the front of the room freely, looking at us, talking to us, and putting his energy and ideas out into the room. As he mentioned a particular explorer, a picture of that person suddenly appeared on the screen. The teacher did not fuss with any equipment, nor did he even turn to look at the screen as he continued his remarks. (He had a wireless control in one hand.) As he mentioned other individuals associated with this personage, their pictures swooped in to encircle the main figure.

As the topic moved on, the screen images vanished completely, and Dr. Bisno spoke of a geographical adventure. A map appeared on the screen, and the speaker stood close to it so he could point to relevant features and indicate routes. Once that was finished, the image disappeared, and Dr. Bisno continued with his remarks.

Moving on to the summary, a series of bullet points appeared sequentially on the screen that summed up the main accomplishments of the explorer. Dr. Bisno let us read the list in silence and then asked us to discuss which points we thought would last in history.

I reflected on how nicely balanced the information was between the spoken and visual forms, how they supplemented each other and the speaker. I noticed that I was never bored or confused and that I felt enriched by the experience. I wished that other people could present as well as Dr. Bisno.

It got me thinking about all the really bad presentations I had suffered through, talks that were made deadly by the inept use of slides. I thought also of the number of people who have come to me with their many slides and no clue how to use them, other than stand there and read them to the audience.

Because wall-to-wall slide usage has become so ubiquitous, you just might think that that is the only way to present information. Vince was just finishing his PhD in American Native Studies. He was going to present his first paper to his academic community. It was crucial to his beginning career that he make an impressive presentation. Vince did not know how to be impressive because he had only seen the usual runthrough of jam-packed word slides in his department. Vince truly needed someone from the outside to break out of this dreary formula. But to do so also involved defying the conventions of his academic community. He needed new options.

If you are a speaker who must present spoken language and visual images, modern presentation products offer you incredible illustrative flexibility. These modern visual aids are supposed to *supplement*, not *substitute* your thoughts and remarks. And therein lies a problem. In many of the presentations that you are likely to see, the slides have come to dominate the presentation, sometimes with dazzling effects that reduce the speaker to a voice in the shadows. The abuse and overuse of PowerPoint is becoming more evident. There are companies that will no longer allow their employees to use this technique because it eats up both preparation and delivery time and has served only to demean the message.

Since you haven't been in Dr. Bisno's class to witness contemporary slide usage, let me describe for you some of the elements that will give you and Vince a more nuanced and balanced presentation at your next opportunity.

The Opening

The British felt it was their mandate to bring Christianity to the nineteenth-century world. What were the consequences of this mission? And do we call that "success" today?

The opening statement needs to grab attention, tweak the imagination, and ask the listeners to care about your topic. As my friend Patricia Fripp, noted speaker and executive coach, says, "Come out punching!" At the beginning of a talk, listeners are deciding if they are going to pay any attention to you. You catch their attention by your intriguing opening statement, not through a slide with a title. You want their focus to be on you and you do not want to compete with a slide.

Note: To tell the truth, many of you actually *do* want your audience to attend to anything but you. You *love* PowerPoint as a crutch and as a way to deal with your stage fright. I do understand. But I intend to make you better and more comfortable *speakers*, not slide readers.

The Material

Consider the information that you want to present and make a decision about the best way to do so, from the audience's point of view. Some material is best just spoken directly.

Some content requires visual display with no commentary, and some is best presented with an interaction of speaking and showing. A mix of these three modes makes for an interesting presentation.

I suggest that you go through your material and edit ruthlessly. (Obviously there is a lot of variation in the need for visual material; a medical pathologist is going to want a non-stop flow of relevant, laboratory images that might illustrate the progress of pathology, for example, and that would be appropriate.) If it reinforces your presentation or illustrates a point in a simple and clear way, keep it.

Never use slides as your notes. Ask yourself if the slide is for *your* benefit or for the audience's. In my opinion, the following points sum up best use of slides:

> *Good*: pictures, bar graphs, charts, maps, attention-grabbing color, video clips
>
> *Bad*: small print, many words, dense data better suited for a handout

Any word slide should have just a few items concisely presented. Use no more than six lines per slide and six words per line. Use upper- and lowercase letters big enough for people in the back to see. Vow that you will *never* have to apologize to your audience for an illegible slide.

And you do not need to enter entire sentences. For example, instead of writing "Our revenues have grown 20%," you could write "Revenues up 20%." In PowerPoint, less is more! Small amounts of text can be useful to create a schema, which is a mental framework for managing the information being provided by the speaker. The speaker verbally fleshes out the information within the schema.

The Noncompete Principle

Allow the audience the time to read your material by themselves. Do not compete with yourself by orally reading your slides to your audience. It is beyond boring! We know that if feeds of information coming through two sensory channels are exactly the same, one becomes irrelevant or extraneous. The audience will choose which one to follow—and it will usually be the visual channel. They will choose NOT to listen to you. This is not what we want.

By watching their eyes, you can tell when your audience is finished reading. Then you can speak in elaboration of a particular point, broaden and amplify the core message, ask for specific questions, make an introductory or summary statement, and by all means, blank the slide by hitting the "B" key when you move to another topic.

This same principle applies to your handout material. If you want people to see a lot of material, data, etc., or to read content, pass it out in paper form *after* your talk when they can attend to it more carefully (unless you like to see people reading while you speak).

The Delivery

We have all witnessed a presentation sabotaged by inept handling of audio-video equipment. Here is the opening of a speech that the president of a professional organization gave over fifty years ago:

> I hope this microphone works. If you have to listen
> to me I hope you can hear me. Once before at a
> gathering of a learned society, seeing an upright
> gadget before me, I talked with extreme care directly
> into it for half an hour, moving neither to the right
> nor to the left, only to find as I went down from the
> platform that it was a *lamp*.

Okay, that's an embarrassment. But there's something about a guy crouching on the floor in front of his waiting audience, testing power sources, adjusting focus, moving furniture, and cursing at his laptop that has the speaker starting from a losing position. If this speaker had any pretention to dignity, presence, and gravitas, it has just been sacrificed.

You just know that David Bisno made darned sure that his visual materials were ready to go long before the lecture so he could look as good as he did. Always come early to test and adjust your equipment. Have everything booted up and have the presentation up and ready. You will look and feel professional with a smooth beginning and will have a much more relaxed presentation.

Try to start and finish your talk with no visuals, demonstrating that *you* are the important element. Let the blank screen be your de facto state with images called upon when needed. Keep the lights up on you so you are never a voice from the shadows. What do *you* do when the lights are turned down, especially after lunch or dinner? Probably the same thing I do—take a little nap.

Always face your audience and speak to them directly. You wouldn't turn your back on someone in a one-on-one conversation. You should not have to turn around to look at the screen to see what is there. You should *know* what is there because you have your laptop screen facing you. Also, facing the big screen means that you are projecting your voice into the back wall, not out into your audience where the ears are. Facing your audience also greatly increases your intelligibility because your speaking is fully available to their ears and eyes, plus it helps you maintain a sense of relationship with them.

Let the screen go blank whenever you can. (Use the "B" key to turn the screen black and the "W" to turn the screen white. If you want the image back, press the buttons again.) Your audience needs a break from the stream of images, and this also lets you get control of their attention. You can allow discussion, invite questions, or simply present your own verbal material with more presence.

Another way to break up the stream of slides is to walk over to the screen, stand beside it (still facing the audience), and point to items of interest with the hand closest to the screen.

Or you can put yourself right in the image, pointing at particular elements to emphasize a point. This dramatically illustrates the fact that the image is serving you and you are not intimidated by a slide.

Use a remote control so you can be mobile during the presentation.

Always rehearse your talk with your visuals in front of some people. This has a huge benefit for you in two important ways:

1. You can detect the flaws in your material, the slides that can be omitted, the information that was not included, and any glitches in the flow of ideas. It's nice to discover these before your actual presentation. Practicing out loud helps you really externalize and evaluate your material in a way that just visual scanning cannot.

2. You will become familiar with the podium, the electronics, the timing, the lighting, and the microphone. As a result, your talk is smooth. This is also a great way to make sure you speak in the time allocated to you.

There is something about the ratta-tat-tat of a flow of bullet slides that is cold and mind numbing. Too much information, not enough meaning. People will prefer a narrative flow, and the human element of storytelling sometimes gives them just the tool for understanding the meaning of your material.

Tell a Story

Nobody can resist a story. David, a radiologist, was to present at a national convention for the first time. He had been developing a new diagnostic visualizing technique. Physicians in his field, typically heavy slide users, would routinely turn off the lights, turn on the slides, and talk with their back to the audience. This was the only style of presentation that David had ever seen, and he was prepared to do the same. Most of his presentation sounded like the following excerpt: "L5-Sl grade IV spondylolistheses, the problem is L5 vertebral body is about 100 percent subluxed over the S1 body; the goal is to reduce this deformity by translating the L5 vertebral body back into its normal position over S1; the problem is that the L5 nerve root can be compressed and or stretched during this reduction process."

Now there is absolutely nothing wrong with this professional instructional language, of course. But David wanted to use this speaking opportunity to show his stuff and ignite his career. Was there anything he could do within this medical context to have a memorable presentation?

I asked him to tell me about some of his clinical cases and I found just what I was looking for: a story that would make sense of his data, make his listeners care about his work, draw them into his presentation, and keep their attention throughout.

David started his narrative just standing beside the podium, telling the story of Mickey, a little boy who was getting progressively weaker and could no longer run with other children. David discussed traditional radiographic diagnostic approaches and showed how those results pertained to Mickey. He used slides to show Mickey's X-rays and test data. Then he turned it off and opened the floor to questions about his results. He asked his audience what they would do at this point. (They loved that question!) After this period, he resumed his talk about the new technique and was able to show how his technique revealed new and useful information about Mickey's condition, information that led to new treatment options. He finished with slides showing a radiant Mickey and his family playing together, followed by another discussion period about his method.

Question: what did his colleagues ask about after the talk? Answer: Mickey. Another question from his fellow doctors: would he be available to deliver this talk at other venues? Answer: you bet!

The moral of the story: PowerPoint data does not stick. Stories do. Most areas of scientific interest are focused on objective data, and this is appropriate for scientific purposes. But for human purposes, we need to have the human narrative. Audiences are human. This is about two-way communication. Here is what I want you to remember:

- When in doubt about the usefulness of a slide, dump it.
- Never show a slide that people cannot easily read.
- Never read a slide to your audience.
- Be a speaker (as opposed to a slide reader).
- Have as few slides as possible.
- Use mostly graphics for your slides.

For more advanced treatment of the use of slides in a presentation, please take a look at the book *slide:olo*gy mentioned in the reference section. Richard Floyd is an IT professional employed by a major healthcare organization, had this to say about the book:

> *Slide:ology* makes me think about the message I'm trying to deliver and how best to convey that message to my audience, before I ever sit down at my computer and open Powerpoint. *Slide:ology* abhors bullet points and welcomes imagery and animation, so when I do open Powerpoint I'm not looking at a blank slide trying to conjure up text lines. *Instead, my imagination is free to run*

wild designing and creating slides that enhance,
support and drive home my already conceived
message to my audience.

It Is the Way You Say It!

"There's many a slip twixt the cup and the lip," we are told. Translating that into communication terms, we might say that the message you intended to send may well not be the message that your listener actually received and considered. Couple that with another communication truism: we are excellent analyzers of the speech and behavior of others, but have very little awareness of our own impact on others. "It's the Way You Say It" is focused on the intersection of these two truths. What we don't know about the way we speak can hurt the effectiveness of our speaking in our work and social worlds. On the other hand, what we are able to bring to awareness and the new skills we are willing to learn can help make us successful communicators indeed.

This is a book about the communication problems of men and women as they experience them in their careers and exactly what was done to help them. It is my hope that others may recognize something like their own concerns on these pages and that they will get a sense of direction for their own improvement.

If You Have Read This Book …

You have probably noticed that the forty-two people whom you meet in this book are perfectly normal and intelligent men and women. There is nothing particularly "wrong" with them. There is just something about the way they speak that causes a problem for them.

Have you noticed how varied the problems are and how they don't usually fit into the listings you might find in the Yellow Pages (such as Public Speaking, Speech Therapy, or

Voice)? Here's a fellow whose perceived "attitude" problem is actually the result of his heavy eyebrows. Here's a lady who must master powerful communication skills to offset the fact that she is tiny and feminine. And here's another—a coxswain—who must learn how to protect her voice as she yells instructions to rowers during fierce competition. These issues are extremely important in the lives of these individuals. There has never been a source of help for the communication problems as experienced by these average citizens until this book. I want to give hope to people who have struggled alone with their speaking concerns, and I want to give them some insight into the process of change so that they can experience success in achieving their speaking goals.

Have you noticed how important it is to have a specific diagnosis of the exact behavior involved in the problem? One lady is deemed "too excitable" for sales calls because her hands and forehead are in constant motion. A minister cannot be heard in the sanctuary because she reads her sermon directly down into the pulpit instead of talking with her congregation. An educated but foreign-born gentleman has a miserable time finding employment because he does not produce certain sounds correctly. Correct identification of the problem leads to appropriate intervention techniques and the possibility of real improvement.

Have you noticed how often I have encouraged regular deliberate practice? Accurate diagnosis is essential, but that alone usually does not change the behavior patterns of speaking. Change requires determined and deliberate repetition of the corrected patterns. There is no other feature more important than individuals' prolonged efforts to improve performance. If you can give this kind of commitment, you can do anything.

What I Have Learned

I have learned how tremendously relieved people are when they get an objective and professional description of their speaking, in contrast to the judgmental and pejorative labels they are likely to have heard. For example, you may have heard from others that you sound like you are lacking in confidence, while I might tell you that you usually do not bring your pitch down at the end of a declarative sentence. What a difference! The first example just makes you feel bad; the second one indicates what you need to do. This professional information is immensely comforting to people. It gives them concrete guidance, which is tremendously liberating for them.

I have learned that people usually take speaking for granted. Most people have not been exposed to the fascinating information that is the professional tool of the speech pathologist. To actively participate in speech improvement exercises, the intelligent adult really has to understand the speech changing process and how it all works. Individuals become aware of the subterranean elements of speech, from learning theory, to the mysteries of neurology, to their own personal structure and development. Understanding why they are doing particular speech patterns greatly adds to the motivation to comply with practice requirements.

Educating the client about speech also provides the opportunity to share its mysteries. There is much to dazzle and astonish the average person. I draw an iceberg, small pointy top, great bulbous mass under the water. Pointing to the small portion protruding above the water, I tell the client, "That is how much the average person knows about communication."

Drawing a line somewhat below the first line illustrates what additional knowledge I, as a trained speech pathologist, bring to the subject. Included in that knowledge is my awareness of how much is *not* known about human communication, illustrated by that great mass under the surface. This is the miracle aspect of speech, a topic that has intrigued numerous thinkers over hundreds of years. It remains elusive, enticing, and never boring.

A Final Word

You have surely glimpsed the subtle and intimate nuances of interpersonal communication, as we have examined our capacity to send and interpret vocal and gestural signals. We have drilled deep and gotten very personal. We have frequently had to face the most emotional and animal aspects of our communication. The unspoken counterpart of this face-to-face intimacy is the incomplete and disembodied communication of the computer. One might be tempted to hide behind the impersonal forms of communication offered by technology to deliberately avoid eye contact and the immediacy of the spoken word. For all the efficiencies of digital communication, it is not the stuff of genuine human interaction.

"The immediate physical presence of other human beings lends great depth and texture to verbal exchanges," Daniel Menaker reminds us. "E-mail and telephone communications don't speak body language, they don't emit pheromones, they can't convey the specific sounds of silences, they take place no place, they cannot involve touch."

I am not alone in my unease with the ubiquity of electronic communication. In his commencement address to the graduating class of the University of Pennsylvania in May 2009, Eric Schmidt, chairman and CEO of Google, urged college graduates to step away from the virtual world and make human connections. "Turn off your computer. You're actually going to have to turn off your phone and discover all that is human around us." And what is most human is spoken language.

This book is my personal contribution to the appreciation of the great miracle of speaking. I hope with all my heart that you have glimpsed this miracle and never stop your study and development of our unique communication repertoire.

I cede the last words to a poet, Walt Whitman:

> Surely whoever speaks to me in the right voice,
> him or her I shall follow,
> As the water follows the moon, silently
> with fluid steps, anywhere around the globe.

Resources

Hearing Yourself as Others Hear You

At the beginning of the university speech and voice courses I taught, I would routinely record each of my twenty students saying the Pledge of Allegiance in random order. This is a passage that everyone could recite without reading it. They were not to identify themselves during the recording. I would then play the recording several days later, asking the students to raise their hand when they thought they heard their own voice. Few could actually identify the sound of their own voice! We rarely get the opportunity to hear our speaking in the context of other voices when we do not know for sure that it is our voice. There is much to be learned from this exercise!

If you are really interested in finding out how you sound when you talk to people, you need to hear your own voice in the same way they hear your voice. This means recording your speech (step one) and actually listening to it (step two). Many people neglect step two due to tremendous reluctance. I think that there is a profound emotional shock when you are listening to yourself. You are using that great auditory analyzing ability you've been developing all your life and turning it on yourself. Switching from internal to external listening can be quite disconcerting and shocking as you realize that your version of your voice is radically different from the one everyone else is hearing. Some people turn the recording machine off so fast that they never get to hear that *they are a lot better than they think they are*. This would be a really good thing to know.

The sound of our voice emanates from the interior of our bodies, and so it represents our unique internal dimensions. What could be more personal? By just listening to a snippet of a voice, you can usually tell if the speaker is a child, a woman, or a man. The way you shape your vowels, the timing of your speech sounds and their completeness, how you shift the melody of your voice, and even how you shape the beginning and end of your syllables are personal characteristics that form your acoustic identity.

Rachel, a job seeker, wanted to change her Southern accent. As far as I was concerned, her accent was soft and pleasant and presented no problems. I recorded our conversation, played it back, and asked her to point out exactly what was objectionable to her. She immediately cried out, "Shut it off! I hate that! It's just a redneck hillbilly!" That is exactly what she heard in her voice, the sound of uneducated people who lived in simple poverty. She *assumed* that the rest of us could picture her background as easily as she could just by hearing the sound of her voice. And she insisted that we find *something* to change. So we did. I identified certain diphthongs (vowel sounds that involve the gliding from one position to another, as in the word "I" [ah-ee]). This gliding did not occur when she used this word, so this was new knowledge for her. She loved it! She'd waltz into my office proclaiming, "I like to fly kites!" gliding through the changes in the vowel like a pro. This was enough for Rachel to feel that she had done something about her accent problem. And she had.

There are many things you *can* do to develop a better, more satisfying speech and voice. There are many people around you who have done it. In order to work on your communication, you'll need to listen to a recording of yourself. If you don't already have a recorder, spend some time at the counter of your favorite electronics store and get something decent. The better the recording quality, the more accurately you'll be able to hear how you sound to others. I have had much better success with tape recorders than with digital devices in capturing the acoustic spectrum of speech sounds and voice, but upgrades in digital devices are happening all the time. Next, record yourself in natural but professional conversation. If possible, record your end of the conversation while you're speaking to a client, colleague, or supervisor on the phone. Ideally, you'll be able to record for at least ten minutes. Why so long? Because the twists and turns of our verbal communication are various and complex.

There is much to be considered: You may be speaking clearly and deliberately for one minute and then swoop into a high-speed mumble as you get excited. You may find that you slip and call someone "honey" when it is inappropriate, or you use other inappropriate language. You could hear that the way you laugh is quite loud and explosive. If you tend to interrupt people, you could catch it on this recording. Or, you may find that your voice has a nice melody that you lose when you get into some prepared language, as in a sales presentation.

You can record a conversation with a friend if necessary, though your vocabulary and other elements of your speech will adjust to this less professional situation and give you a slightly different sample of your speaking. But you do want other people involved.

If you read something out loud, you will not sound the same as when you naturally talk, and if you just try to talk to a recording machine in an otherwise empty room, you will not be using the same speech styling and voice that you do with people. You want to hear your normal, natural speaking voice. Speaking is a social act that comes into being through interaction.

You'll be using this recording in the next chapter to assess your communication on a wide range of characteristics. Remember, it's ultimately up to you to decide which unique vocal traits you will accept and which you'd like to adjust for social and professional reasons. There's no one way to sound, but there is a range of norms that tend to be more acceptable.

Completing a Vocal Self-Evaluation

Have you made a recording? Good! You've now done something positive that will really help you change the sound of your voice. Using this recording, you can complete a self-evaluation that will determine what chapters you'll be focusing on throughout the book. It's best to wait a few hours between making the recording and listening for this self-evaluation, as time will offer you more distance and objectivity. You may need to listen to the recording several times, as you can really only listen for one or two vocal elements at a time. I know how uncomfortable this is for many people. It is simply not something that you ordinarily do. It is something you expressly avoid doing; am I right? I offer the following words of Seneca (Roman philosopher) to encourage you:

> It's not because things are difficult that we don't dare.
> It's because we don't dare that things are difficult.

First just listen to get a sense of this person on the recording without critique. Listen with interest and kindness. You want the big picture and the general impression now. For example: "I sound just like my Mom!" "I'm a lot better than I thought I was!"

With enough listening, certain features will start to catch your attention. Many people are way too critical of their speaking and seek out an abundance of imagined flaws. Ask yourself if you would be that critical if you were listening to the speech of another person. If this seems like an overwhelming task to you, just use the following check list to help guide your listening.

Your Checklist

Check no more than three of the issues you noticed while listening (or that people have regularly told you are a problem for you). You'll use this information, along with the evaluations from others, to help determine where you really need to focus your efforts:

_____ My vocabulary could be more professional.

_____ I use too many fillers (um, like, you know, etc.).

_____ I talk too much.

_____ I talk too little.

_____ My voice is too loud.

_____ My voice is too soft.

_____ My accent is difficult to understand.

_____ I speak too fast.

_____ I speak too slowly.

_____ My voice is too high.

_____ My voice is too low.

_____ I don't articulate words clearly.

_____ My voice is raspy/creaky.

_____ My voice is monotone.

_____ My voice is too effusive (pitch changes too much).

_____ My voice seems young/immature.

_____ My voice is challenging to listen to.

_____ My speaking is staccato (syllables are punchy, choppy).

_____ My tone of voice seems too flirty for a professional environment.

_____ My voice starts out strong but fades at the end of sentences.

_____ My sentences end with a questioning tone, even
when making a statement.

_____ I don't sound confident while speaking.

_____ I struggle to get the point across succinctly;
I ramble.

Many of us find that it's difficult to evaluate ourselves with
confidence, and we turn to other people for their opinion. In
the next section, I will give you a similar evaluation form to
give to others for this feedback. This will be very helpful, but
it requires some careful thought.

Getting External Feedback on Your Communication

Getting the opinions of a few trustworthy people about your
communication can greatly help you improve your skills.
After all, you're trying to improve the way you come across to
others, so the opinion of others should be respected. You are
going to look for areas of consensus, as not everyone is equally
skilled at offering accurate feedback on these matters.

Again, making yourself vulnerable to the opinion of others
may be a great test of your courage. Consider another point of
view: what would you think of someone who sought out your
opinion of their communication skills and specifically asked
for your advice? I'll tell you how you'd feel: honored, trusted,
and respected. And what would your opinion of that person
be? You would respect them for their courage, seriousness of
purpose, and positive attitude (and secretly you would wish
you had their guts!).

Offer this questionnaire to two or three different people
whom you like and respect, and also who you think will answer
you honestly. If you can consult a colleague or a supervisor

for this, it would be immensely helpful to hear how you are presenting yourself professionally from their point of view.

Note: Make it very clear that you are asking for specific feedback about your communication skills. *Many people will be reluctant to comment if they fear hurting your feelings.* If you are from a different culture, they may be concerned about some kind of "discrimination complaint." Use your intuition and offer such people reassurance that they will be assisting you in developing better communication skills that will really help you advance. I refer to these people as your "external ears," people in a position to give you helpful feedback.

A speech specialist is also a good option for this kind of feedback. (Consult www.vasta.org for such a person in your area. Go to www.asha.org if you desire the more advanced training of a speech pathologist.) Once you compare your self-evaluation with the feedback from several others, you can decide which areas to focus on using the exercises and guidance in this book.

Communication Evaluation

[*Insert your name here*] is asking for your opinion about his/ her communication effectiveness. Please fill out this form honestly and constructively. Your responses will help guide the person who gave it to you (referred to as the subject) in determining which communication areas he/she is succeeding in and which could use more practice and improvement. The subject wants to make sure he/she is communicating effectively and accurately, and needs to know how he/she is actually coming across to others. (Often we don't know how we sound, and we need others to let us know.) Unless told otherwise, please treat this information as confidential.

For each comment below, please answer "Yes," "No," or "Some." Feel free to comment as needed.

_____ Subject could benefit from a more appropriate professional vocabulary.

_____ Subject uses too many fillers (um, like, you know, etc.).

_____ Subject talks too much.

_____ Subject talks too little.

_____ Subject's voice is too loud.

_____ Subject's voice is too soft.

_____ Subject's accent is difficult to understand.

_____ Subject speaks too fast.

_____ Subject speaks too slowly.

_____ Subject's voice is too high.

_____ Subject's voice is too low.

_____ Subject doesn't articulate words clearly.

_____ Subject's voice is raspy/creaky.

_____ Subject's voice is monotone.

_____ Subject's voice is too effusive (pitch changes too much).

_____ Subject's voice seems young/immature.

_____ Subject's voice is challenging to listen to. Please explain.

_____ Subject's speaking is staccato (seems punchy or aggressive).

_____ Subject's tone of voice can seem too flirty for the professional environment.

_____ Subject's voice starts out strong but fades at the end of sentences.

_____ Subject ends sentences with a questioning tone, even when making a statement.

_____ Subject usually doesn't seem confident while speaking.

_____ Subject's body language doesn't usually fit with what's being said.

_____ Subject doesn't make appropriate eye contact.

_____ Subject often doesn't seem to be listening or interested in what others say.

_____ Subject often seems distant or disrespectful to others.

_____ Subject doesn't make a strong first impression.

_____ Subject struggles to get the point across.

_____ Subject undersells talents and skills.

_____ Subject seems to struggle with small talk.

Other constructive feedback:

Acknowledgments

It was good to know that you were in my corner,
dear friends. Your belief and personal efforts on my behalf
have meant more to me than I can say here.

So here I say simply, thank you, Jill Marsal,
Ursula Kauth, Colleen Wilcox, and Bonnie Stuppin.

Notes

"The Art of Conversation; Chattering Classes." *The Economist.* December 19, 2006.

Brown, Willie. *Basic Brown.* New York: Simon & Schuster; Reprint edition, 2011.

Gladwell, Malcolm. *Outliers: The Story of Success.* New York: Little, Brown and Co., 2008.

Fine, Debra. *The Fine Art of Small Talk.* Englewood: Small Talk Pub., 2004. (A useful and comprehensive guide in the how-to genre)

Ericsson, K. Anders, Ralf Th. Krampe, and Clemens Tesch-Romer. "The Role of Deliberate Practice in the Acquisition of Expert Performance." *Psych. Review,* Vol. 100 (1993).

Fisher, Hilda. *Improving Voice and Articulation.* Boston: Houghton Mifflin Co., 1975.

James, Henry. *A Question of Our Speech.* Boston and New York: Houghton Mifflin, 1905. (Speech to graduating class at Bryn Mawr College, June 1905.)

Gilbert, Frederick. *Speaking Up: Surviving Executive Presentations.* Redwood City: PSI, 2012.

MacNeil, Robert, and William Cran. *Do You Speak American?* New York: Doubleday, 2005.

Menaker, Daniel. *A Good Talk.* New York: Twelve, 2010.

Minto, Barbara. *The Pyramid Principle.* Third edition. London: Prentice Hall, 2002.

Sikorski, Lorna. *Intonation Patterns of American English.* Tustin: LDS & Associates, 2005.

Walters, Barbara. *How to Talk with Practically Anybody about Practically Anything.* Garden City: Doubleday & Company, Inc., 1970. (While fascinating in terms of the content, it also demonstrates how graciousness and compassion are important elements of social conversation. You'll have to look for this one in the used-book section.)

Williamson, Marianne. *A Return to Love: Reflections on the Principles of "A Course in Miracles."* New York: Harper Perennial, 1996. (The quoted passage is frequently misidentified as the 1994 inaugural speech of Nelson Mandela.)

A Note about the Author's Other Publications

The Sound of Your Voice, the audio self-improvement series, and *The Serious Business of Small Talk* are available on audiotape or CD and can be purchased through Dr. Fleming's website, Speechtraining.com.

Index

About the Author

"I help people understand the impression they make by the way they speak," says Carol Fleming. "I show them what they are doing that is just fine and where they could improve, if they want to." As simple as this may sound on the surface, the outcomes are multitudinous and varied. Carol's career as a personal communication coach is centered in San Francisco, but her audio series, *The Sound of Your Voice, the Serious Business of Small*

Photo: Grace Image Photography

Talk, and her book, *It's the Way You Say It*, have carried her work around the world. She regularly works with people on Skype and currently has clients in the Dominican Republic, Cyprus, and Boston: multitudinous and varied, indeed.

Carol enjoys singing with the San Francisco Choral Society and has been on the Board of Directors of the Commonwealth Club of California for over twenty years. Her home is shared by two cats, Milly Piccadilly and Bill Bonney, and an aquarium full of South American cichlids.

Dr. Fleming earned her PhD from Northwestern University in the Department of Communication Disorders.

Berrett–Koehler
Publishers

Berrett-Koehler is an independent publisher dedicated to an ambitious mission: *Creating a World That Works for All*.

We believe that to truly create a better world, action is needed at all levels—individual, organizational, and societal. At the individual level, our publications help people align their lives with their values and with their aspirations for a better world. At the organizational level, our publications promote progressive leadership and management practices, socially responsible approaches to business, and humane and effective organizations. At the societal level, our publications advance social and economic justice, shared prosperity, sustainability, and new solutions to national and global issues.

A major theme of our publications is "Opening Up New Space." Berrett-Koehler titles challenge conventional thinking, introduce new ideas, and foster positive change. Their common quest is changing the underlying beliefs, mindsets, institutions, and structures that keep generating the same cycles of problems, no matter who our leaders are or what improvement programs we adopt.

We strive to practice what we preach—to operate our publishing company in line with the ideas in our books. At the core of our approach is stewardship, which we define as a deep sense of responsibility to administer the company for the benefit of all of our "stakeholder" groups: authors, customers, employees, investors, service providers, and the communities and environment around us.

We are grateful to the thousands of readers, authors, and other friends of the company who consider themselves to be part of the "BK Community." We hope that you, too, will join us in our mission.

A BK Life Book

This book is part of our BK Life series. BK Life books change people's lives. They help individuals improve their lives in ways that are beneficial for the families, organizations, communities, nations, and world in which they live and work. To find out more, visit **www.bk-life.com**.